Introduction to Chronobiology

Mrs. Gauri R. Sathaye

Dr. Prashant S. Duraphe

S.P. Mandali's

Late Prin. B. V. Bhide Foundation, Pune
411030

ISBN: 978-81-956253-0-7

Publisher:
Dr. Radhika Inamdar
Secretary, Shikshana Prasaraka Mandali,
Sadashiv Peth, Pune 411030

Edition: First, 2022

Website:
www.bhidefoundation.org
www.chronoprakriti.com

Price:
Rs. 300-00

Disclaimer:
The information in this book has been compiled by way of general guidance in relation to the specific subject addressed, but it is not a substitute and not to be relied on for medical, healthcare or other professional advice on specific circumstances and in specific locations. Please consult your physician before changing, stopping or starting any medical treatment. The authors and publishers disclaim, as far as the law allows, any liability arising directly or indirectly from the use and misuse of the information contained in this book.

Preface

It has been over four years that a Nobel Prize in Physiology or Medicine (2017) was awarded to Jeffrey C. Hall, Michael Rosbash and Michael W. Young which brought the field of 'chronobiology' to the center stage in the scientific and academic world. The fascinating discoveries of biological clocks giving rise to various rhythmic processes in organisms as diverse as tiny bacteria to giant mammals and plants have dotted the scientific world since 18th century. The field has advanced in recent times and newer discoveries are being reported at a greater pace. However there are very few textbooks consolidating the advances in chronobiology for bachelors and masters students.

I am happy to see a much needed textbook which introduces this field at the college level. From basic concepts and definitions to the recent advances and applications of chronobiology in various fields, the textbook gives an excellent overview of various aspects of the field. Appropriate illustrations, diagrams and glossary of important concepts add to the clarity and quality of the content.

The authors have taken great efforts to bring a simple and interesting account of a relatively new and emerging field for students and teachers. This book will also be a good resource material for enthusiasts, curious citizens and scientists who would like to dive deeper into the fascinating world of biological clocks.

Dr. Dhanashree Paranjpe
Evolutionary Biologist

CONTENTS

ACKNOWLEDGMENTS

We would like acknowledge all our students who motivated us for writing this book and well-wishers who directly or indirectly helped in this endeavor. We would like to express our sincere gratitude towards Savardekar family (Shailesh, Manjusha, Yuga) for their active participation in cover page design, drawing diagrams as well as coordinating with publishers. We are thankful to Mrs. Avantika Sathaye Dandekar and Mr. Saurabh Sathaye for their help in typing and drafting. Dr. Meenal Joshi, Director of Late Prin. B .V .Bhide foundation is a source of inspiration from the beginning who along with Mrs. Manjusha Savardekar involved in multiple proof readings and providing inputs in the form of chapter wise exercises. At the end, we would like to thank Shikshana Prasaraka Mandali, Pune for providing us the platform to publish the book on the relatively unknown but relevant topic of Chronobiology.

PART I

OVERVIEW OF BIOLOGICAL TIMEKEEPING

1 CONCEPT AND SCOPE

Chronobiology or circadian biology is a relatively new branch of science. Chronobiology deals with the relationship between time and biological functions. It also studies how natural rhythms affect living organisms. All people are subject to natural daily rhythms that affect our biology. This is true not just for humans, but for almost all living organisms and it affects various aspects of biological functioning.

Chronobiology is a word derived from three Greek stems: 'Chronos' for time, 'bios' for life and 'logos' for study. Webster's dictionary defines "time" as the measured or measurable period during which an action process or condition exists or continues. Webster defines the word "timing" as selection for maximum effect of the precise moment for beginning or doing something. These concepts of "time", "timing" as well as "clock" and "rhythm" are key characters in chronobiology. Chronobiology studies variations of the timing and duration of biological activity in living organisms which occur for many essential biological processes.

Chronobiology comprises the systematic scientific study of living timing processes in plants, animals and microorganisms. This field deals with living internal clocks that track and help anticipate important environmental rhythmic events. In other words, chronobiology is a study of rhythmic variations of most biological variables. The field of chronobiology is dynamic, fascinating and rapidly expanding around the world. It can help explain why birds migrate, why trees drop their leaves in fall and even why some medications should only be taken at particular time of the day.

World's most reliable time keeper, the sun provides daily light and temperature changes and also sets our biological clock. This biological clock ultimately controls our daily, monthly and seasonal behavior. Not only at behavioural level but the biological clock is also responsible for the coordination of our physiological rhythms. Thus, biological clocks are elegant adaptive strategies that avoid the problems of mere passive responses of organisms to changes in the environment. Many animals and plants seem to be able to respond to environmental events before they even occur. For instance, many animals that are active during the day come out just before the sun rises. Plants can anticipate the sunrise orienting their leaves towards the horizon before the sun actually rises. Likewise plants that exhibit sleep movements tend to "wake up" (raise their leaves) a little before sunrise.

The field of chronobiology studies various biological rhythms in living organisms and how they are tuned by cues from the outside world such as day-night cycle due to rotation of earth. Chronobiological research is predominantly directed towards the elucidation of the relation between biological rhythms and environmental periodicity.

Like most processes within organisms have time profiles, the majority of the interactions between organisms and their environment have distinct temporal profiles. The study of wild clocks will be an intense area of research in the ecology once chronobiological experimental tools would be validated for field studies.

Chronobiological understanding can be effectively applied in agricultural activities. Use of weedicides or pesticides can be used effectively by understanding the rhythmicity of weeds or pests so as to reduce the impact on soil or crop. Similarly yield of commercial crops can be optimized by following the rhythmic pattern of most of the physiological processes in plant life cycle.

Human microbiome also follows a rhythmic pattern which assists in metabolic functions. Our large eating window is disturbing the microbial rhythmicity thus leading to metabolic disorders such as obesity or diabetes. Understanding of microbial clock will provide many important insights into the evolution of clock mechanism as well as handling many of the lifestyle disorders.

Temporal understanding of biological processes in the context of various systems such as chronophysiology, chronopharmacology, chronotoxicology and chronotherapy are studied in detail all over the world so as to incorporate chronomedicine into mainstream diagnostic and prognostic procedures. Our modern 24x7 lifestyle does not take biological clock mechanism into account and thus leads to mismatch between internal clock and external clock which is the major concern and root cause of most of the lifestyle disorders.

Sleep and psychological disorders would be effectively managed by chronobiological perspective. Circadian dysfunction affects the majority of vital processes including sleep or depression. Circadian lifestyle choices will prove effective without medical intervention for most of the disorders that we face today. Sleep can effectively set our biological clock. Consistent sleep-wake timing may be first line treatment for majority of health issues we face today. Sleep science is an integral part of chronobiology which cannot be differentiated from each other.

Age-old Ayurvedic concepts such as *Dinacharya* (day schedule), *Ratricharya* (night schedule) *Ritucharya* (seasonal schedule), and *Prakriti* types (Body compositions) could be revisited with modern chronobiological concepts. Personalized medicine would be more effective through the combination of

Ayurvedic & Chronotherapeutic approaches. For example, *Dinacharya and Ratricharya* can be explained in terms of circadian rhythm. *Ritucharya,* may be in terms of infradian rhythms and *Prakriti* types may be complimentary concept of Chronotype.

Summary

- Chronobiology is the study of biology of time and internal biological clocks.

- The field of chronobiology studies innate biological rhythms and how they are influenced by external factors.

- Biological rhythms allow organisms to anticipate and adapt cyclic changes in the environment that are caused by the daily rotation of the earth on its axis.

- As organisms have been constantly exposed to periodic changes in the environment, biological clocks in their body anticipate and prepare for the imminent sunrise or sunset and temperature fluctuation.

- Chronopharmacology, Chronomedicine, Sleep science are the major sub-specialties of chronobiology.

Exercise

A] Multiple Choice Questions

1. Chronobiology deals with the relationship between _______ and _____.

    a. Space and biological function
    b. Time and space function
    c. Time and biological function

2. Time, timing, clock and rhythms are key characters of ________.

    a. Pharmacology
    b. Chronobiology
    c. Physiology

3. Daily, monthly and seasonal behaviors are controlled by ________.

    a. Biological clock
    b. External clock
    c. Environmental clock

4. Study of wild clock refers to

    a. Ecological chronobiology
    b. Agricultural chronobiology
    c. Chronomedicine

5. Ayurvedic seasonal rhythms may be experimentally proven with study of

   a. Circadian rhythms

   b. Ultradian rhythms

   c. Infradian rhythms

B] Answer the following

1. Define Chronobiology.

2. Give the importance of biological clocks.

3. What are the possible consequences if there is mismatch between internal and external clocks?

4. Comment on the scope of the field of chronobiology.

C] Activity

Demonstration of the Briggs-Rauscher reaction to explain chemical oscillation.

https://www.instagram.com/p/CZpH7DMJeXv/?utm_medium=share_sheet

Glossary

Biological clock:

Self-sustained oscillators that generate biological rhythms in the absence of external periodic output.

Chronobiology:

The study at all levels of organization of adaptations evolved by living organisms to cope with regularly occurring environmental cycles.

Circadian clock:

The endogenous molecular mechanism which accounts for observable 24 hours circadian rhythm in an organism's activities including locomotion, sleep-wake cycle etc.

Rhythm:

A non-random series of events without any statement of causation.

References

- Textbook of Chronobiology, A. N. Shukla Discovery Publishing House Pvt Ltd New Delhi 2010

- Chronobiology: Biological Timing edited by Dunlap, Loros and DeCoursey, Sinauer associates Inc. 2004

2 HISTORICAL PERSPECTIVE

Introduction

Awareness of daily, lunar and seasonal time in organizing the activities of early humans is as old as human evolution itself. Since the beginning of mankind, human history has been shaped by light and darkness. In early humans, life was dictated by the powerful presence of sun, it's rising and setting. For Paleolithic humans, the sun, moon and stars must have been very important for estimating daily and seasonal time. Paleolithic humans almost certainly read solar shadows to estimate time of day as shown in figure 1.

Similarly the moon was also used in determining seasonal time. Though we are well aware of external clocks, very little knowledge/awareness is present about the inner clock of living things. Many essential biological processes in living organisms include the variations of the timing and duration of biological activities. It was debated for long in scientific world about the endogenous nature of this clock in living systems.

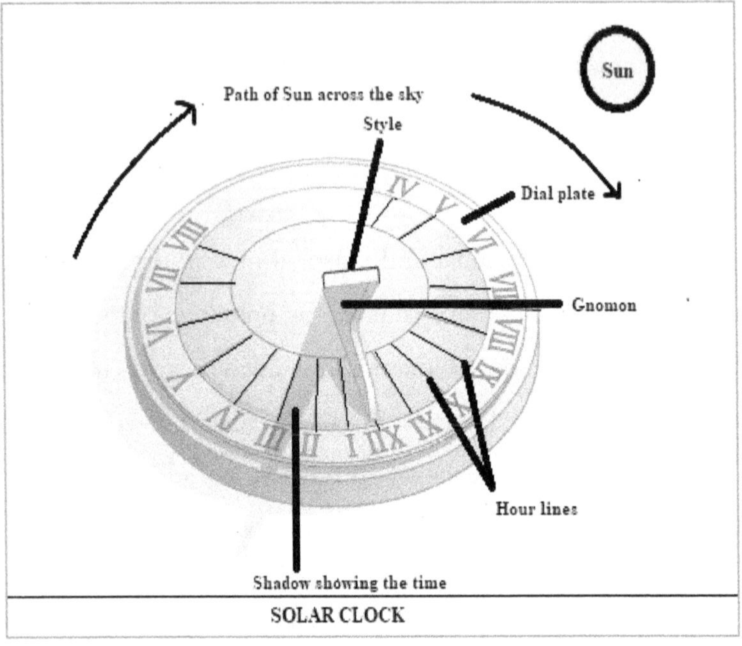

Figure 1: Solar clock - Shadow of sun movement used by Paleolithic humans for measurement of time.

Experimental evidence of endogenous clock

Jean-Jacques d'Ortous de Mairan, a French astronomer was the first to observe the rhythmic behavior of leaves of a *Mimosa* plant. *Mimosa* plant was already known to fold its leaves and leaflets close at night and reopen them during the day. When he placed plants in constant darkness, he found that leaf opening and closing persisted just as if the plants were seeing the day and night as shown in figure 2. With this came the first experimental evidence for the persistence of an endogenous rhythmicity in the absence of environmental cues.

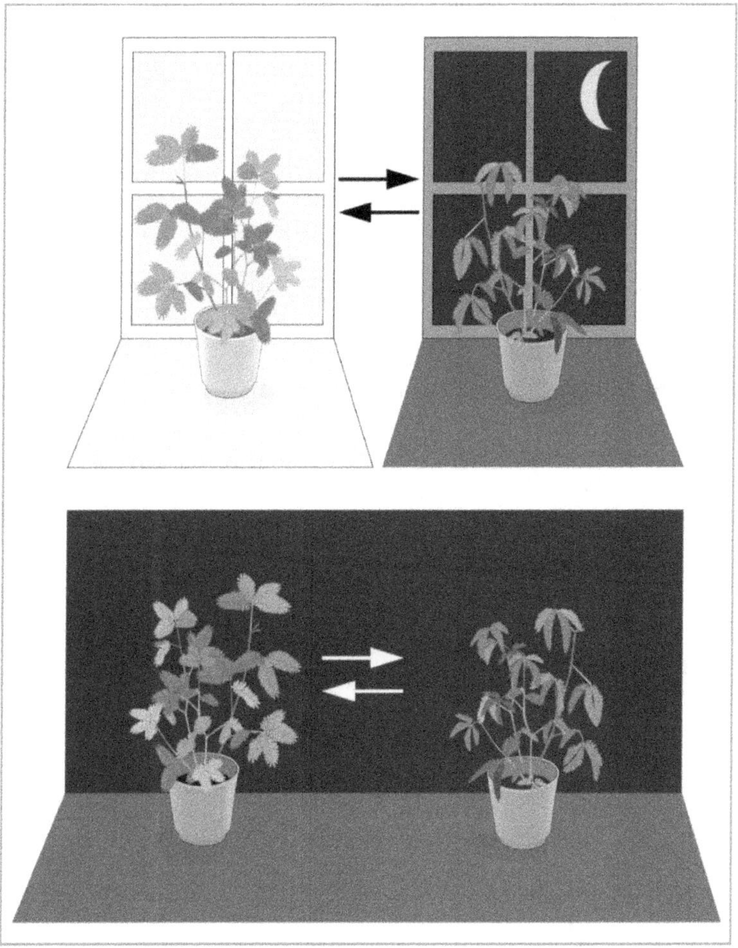

Figure 2: Endogenous biological clock in *Mimosa pudica* - In natural day-night conditions, leaves of *Mimosa* exhibits diurnal rhythm which is persisted even in a 24h dark environment suggesting endogenous nature of circadian rhythmicity in leaf movement. (Adapted from www.nobelprize.org)

This finding suggested that the movement represented something more than a simple response to the sun and was controlled by an internal clock.

In the 1860s Karl Ernst Von Baer wrote about the biological time and its difference in different species of animals. In 1924 Alexander Chizhevsky, published interdisciplinary work: 'Physical factors behind the process of history' and 'Epidemiological catastrophes and periodic activity of the Sun'. In this work he studied cycles in living organisms in connection with the solar cycle and cycle of lunar phases.

The 1960 symposium at Cold Spring Harbor Laboratory seems to define the moment when researchers from widely different fields discovered that they all were studying the same phenomenon. The meeting laid the groundwork for the field of chronobiology. Studies conducted in the 1950s on circadian rhythmicity in fruit flies by Colin Pittendrigh and in humans by Juergen Aschoff can be considered its foundation. These scientists have made substantial contributions and formalizations in the second half of the 20th century. They pursued different but complementary views on the phenomenon of entrainment of the circadian system by light. Thus it wasn't until the 20th century when the chronobiology research truly began.

Wilhelm Pfeffer, Erwin Buenning, Karl Von Frisch, Juergen Aschoff, Colin Pittendrigh, Arthur Winfree and Franz Halberg are among its pioneers. The legacies of these pioneers continue today with the advancement of the fields they founded.

In 2017 the Nobel prize in physiology or medicine was awarded to Jeffrey C. Hall, Michael Rosbash and Michael W. Young for their discoveries of "Molecular mechanisms controlling the circadian rhythm in fruit flies" Application of chronobiological concepts in medicine is slowly gaining momentum and the branch called chronomedicine is getting established which will help in attaining the goal of personalized medicine in future.

Contributions of various scientists in the field of chronobiology is tabulated below which gives an overview of the progress in chronological order so as to understand the time taken by scientific community to accept the presence of endogenous clock. Though the initial observations were made on plants, further research was predominantly carried out on various animal models and plant chronobiology was not progressed much till recent time.

It was surprising that in spite of keen observations of biological rhythmicity in all living systems including humans, it was considered pseudoscience until recently, partly because the term biorhythms is associated with esoteric concepts. Hence it is advised to use the term biological rhythms instead of biorhythms.

Table 1: Milestones in Science of Chronobiology

Name of Scientist	Discovery
Androsthenes (350 BC)	Observed and documented that *Tamarandus indica* exhibit sleep movement
Sanctorious (1657) **Father of autorhythmometry**	Demonstrated for the first time the presence of rhythms in humans by experimenting on self
J.J. de Mairan (1729)	Observed and documented that leaf movement persisted in absence environmental variations
Carolus Linnaeus (1751)	Designed Floral clock based on opening and closing of petals
De Candolle (1832)	Observed and documented that leaf movement of *Mimosa pudica* persisted in constant darkness but differ from 24 hrs

Zehetmeier (1845)	Observed change in urinary volume rhythm in patients with heart disease
Sutherland / Simpson (1863)	Recorded axillary temperature rhythms of rhesus monkeys
Wilhelm Pfeffer (1914)	Documented leaf movement of plant *Flemingia congesta*
J. C. Bose (1927) **First Indian scientist documented rhythmicity**	Demonstrated and documented rhythmic behavior in many plants (*Casia alata, Mimosa pudica, Luffa acutangula*)
Erwin Buenning (1930) **Co-founder of chronobiology**	Demonstrated entrainment of leaf movement rhythm
Colin Pittendrigh (1954) **Co-founder of chronobiology**	Demonstrated temperature compensatory behavior of circadian clocks
Von Frisch & Lindauer (1954)	Demonstrated presence of time sense in honey bees

Franz Halberg (1959) **Founder of Chronomedicine**	Coined the term 'circadian'. Documented long term rhythmicity in blood pressure
Juergen Aschoff (1960) **Co-founder of chronobiology**	Postulated Aschoff's rules about contradictory sensitivity of endogenous circadian system to environmental stimuli for diurnal and nocturnal animals
Buenning, Aschoff, and Pittendrigh **(Landmark Annual symposium of the Cold Spring Harbor Biological Laboratory, 1960)**	Presented a conceptual and experimental framework for the new interdisciplinary field of chronobiology
Hoffmann (1961)	Demonstrated endogenous clock in birds
Ron Konopka (1971) **Founder of molecular chronobiology**	Discovery of first clock gene 'period'
Ehret (1974)	Coined the term "chronotype" as the temporal phenotype of an

	organism which captures a biological trait
Ralph & Menaker (1988)	Experimentally obtained first clock mutant in golden hamster
Joseph Takahashi (1997)	Cloning of clock genes
Jeffery Hall, Michael Rosbach, Michael Young (2017)	Nobel prize in physiology or medicine for molecular mechanism controlling circadian rhythm

Contributions of Indian Scientists

Sir Jagadish Chandra Bose (1858-1937) had made very early and very important contributions to the field of chronobiology and circadian rhythms at a time when neither of the two technical terms had been coined. J. C. Bose, even though a physicist, performed extensive experiments on the responses of plants to light, temperature and other stimuli. His plant physiological researches fill 1122 printed pages of four volumes of monographs published in the year 1918, 1919, 1923 and 1927. He observed and recorded natural phenomena which were further experimentally verified in the laboratory by self-fabricated instruments of elegance and simplicity. The Nyctitropic recorder he used for recording leaf movements is shown in the figure 3.

Figure 3: Nyctitropic recorder designed and manufactured by Prof. JC Bose. In-house developed instrument was used for recordings of leaf movements.

Almost 70 years after **Prof. M. K. Chandrashekaran**, who studied biological rhythms in plants, fruit flies, crabs, mice, bats, squirrels and humans established an active school of research in chronobiology at the Madurai Kamaraj University. After many years he moved to the Jawaharlal Nehru Centre for Advanced Scientific Research (JNCASR) at Bangalore, the unit which had begun with him in 1996. He worked as Honorary Professor in the Evolutionary and Organismal Biology Unit (EOBU) and focused his attention on rhythms in insects. His special area of study was the periodicities associated with endogenous, near-24 hour rhythms that are seen in creatures ranging from blue-green algae to humans.

Prof. Vijay Kumar Sharma did post-doctoral studies in the chronobiology laboratory of Prof M. K. Chandrashekaran at Madurai Kamaraj University in 1995-96. He further joined JNCASR in 1998 as a fellow in Evolutionary and Organismal Biology Unit (EOBU) and became faculty fellow in 1999 and established one of the first *Drosophila* chronobiology laboratories in India. He along with his co-workers empirically tested and validated Pittendrigh's 'Circadian resonance hypotheses' in fruit flies and ants. Since then Prof. Vijay Kumar Sharma remained close collaborator of Prof. Chandrashekaran until his last days EOBU at JNCASR, Bangalore.

Dr. Dilip Joshi was a Researcher at Ahmednagar College, Maharashtra, India where he worked on the oviposition rhythm of fruit fly and guided many students in chronobiology research.

Many other scientists are contributing to chronobiology research all over India. **Prof. Vinod Kumar** (President, Indian Society for Chronobiology, Delhi University), **Prof. Sanjay Kumar Bhardwaj** (Secretary, InSC, Charan Singh University Meerut), **Prof. Sheeba Vasu,** (JNCASR, Bangalore), **Prof. Atanu Kumar Pati**, (Pt. Ravishankar Shukla University School of Studies in Life Science Chronobiology and Animal Behaviour Lab, Raipur), **Prof. Shalie Malik**, (Department of

Zoology, University of Lucknow, Lucknow). **Prof. A. S. Dixit,** (North-Eastern Hill University, Umshing, Mawkynroh, Shillong) are involved in the chronobiology research on various aspects like Avian behaviour and Life history studies, Clock and metabolism using migratory birds as model systems, Lifestyle patterns and biological clock mediated functions in human, Neuronal circuit that regulates rhythmic behaviours such as locomotor activity, sleep, adult-emergence, feeding and egg-laying in *Drosophila*.

The list is not exhaustive and many young scientists and laboratories in India are now working on the temporal regulation of various aspects of biological processes. Indian Society for Chronobiology was established in 1977 which provides a forum for discussion and exchange of ideas among the Indian chronobiologists.

Summary

- The perpetual alteration of night and day could not escape being noticed by the earliest humans. It must have marked to them the passage of time.

- The young science from Europe called Chronobiology has been gaining importance over the past 50 years.

- The field of Chronobiology originated from keen observation of plants and it was not until later that the first observations of endogenously driven rhythms in bacteria, insects, rodents, primates and humans were discovered.

- Chronobiology dates back to 1729 when the French astronomer Jean Jacques d`Ortous de Marian noticed that the leaf movements of the *Mimosa* plant had an endogenous day-night cycle.

- It wasn't until the early 1880s that the concept of an inherited rhythm was theorized.

- Many Indian scientists are involved in basic chronobiology research till date.

Exercise:

A] Multiple Choice Questions

1. De Mairan used _________ plant for his experiment.

    a. Rose
    b. *Asparagus*
    c. *Mimosa*

2. _________ is considered as 'Father Chronomedicine'.

    a. Franz Halberg

   b. De Marian

   c. Erwin Buenning

3. In 2017, the Nobel Prize was awarded to Jeffry C. Hall, Michael Robash and Michael W. Young for their work on ___________.

   a. Butterflies

   b. Fruit flies

   c. Houseflies

4. ________ is the first Indian scientist who demonstrated rhythmic behavior in many plants.

   a. Prof. Vijay Kumar Sharma
   b. Sir J. C. Bose
   c. Prof. Dilip Joshi

5. Hoffman demonstrated an endogenous clock in _________.

   a. Reptiles

   b. Birds

   c. Mammals

B] Answer in one sentence

1. Who coined the word "Circadian"?

2. What is the inference from the experiment carried by De Marian?

3. Write the name of any three Indian scientists who contributed to Chronobiological research.

4. Who is the founder of molecular chronobiology?

C] Activity

Study the floral clock of Linnaeus and observe the blooming time of at least six flower species during the day and draw your own floral clock.

Glossary

Circadian rhythm:

A biological rhythm that persists under conditions of constant environmental factors with a period length of about a day, whose phase can be reset by a brief interruption in the constant regimen, and whose period length is relatively independent of temperature within the physiological range of normal growth.

Chronotype:

The term chronotype is used to describe a psychological personality trait associated with preferred daily times.

References

- M. H. Vitaterna, J. S. Takahashi, and F. W. Turek, "Overview of circadian rhythms" (in eng), Alcohol Res Health, vol. 25, no. 2, pp. 85-93, 2001.

- Chronobiology: Biological Timing edited by Dunlap, Loros and DeCoursey, Sinauer associates Inc. 2004

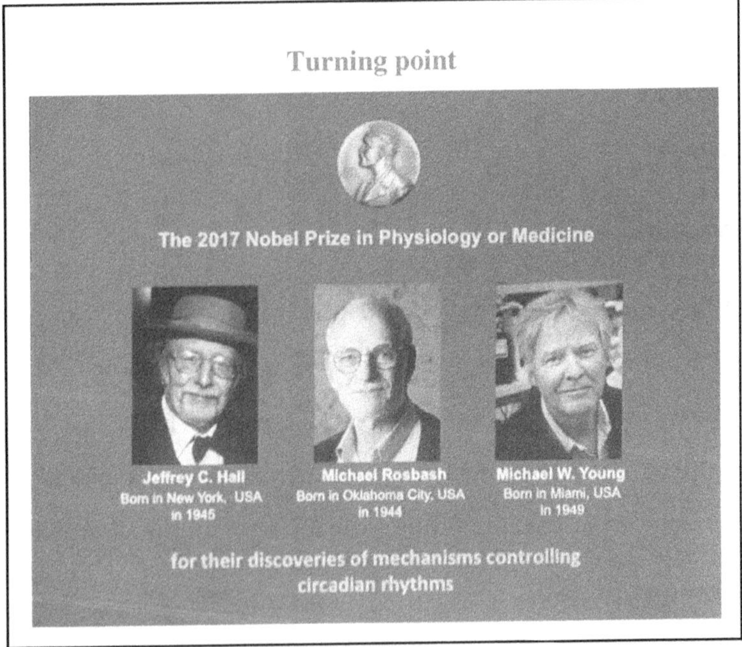

3 GEOPHYSICAL CYCLES

Introduction

The common geophysical cycles of everyday experience can be connected with the rotation of the earth around its axis (solar and lunar diurnal variation) or its rotation around the sun (annual variation). Organisms have evolved to cope with geophysical cycles of different periods of length. Collectively the daily, seasonal lunar and tidal geophysical cycles regulate much of the temporal biology of life on earth as shown in figure 4.

Effect of geophysical cycle on humans

The daily (23 hr. 56 min.), seasonal (365.24 days), lunar (29.53 days) and tidal (12.8 hours) cycles provide the temporal cues. These cues provide coordination in various activities like daily feeding patterns, daily and seasonal migration, growth, reproduction, hibernation and much else. Much of human physiology and behavior is controlled by an internal ~ 24 hour daily timer in anticipation of the varying demands of the day-night cycle. We have an endogenous clock that is locked to the solar day and allows an optional response to the differing demands of the day and night.

We have an endogenous clock that is locked to the solar day and allows an optional response to the differing demands of the day and night. Preferred wake and sleep time are to large extent driven by an endogenous temporal program that uses sunlight.

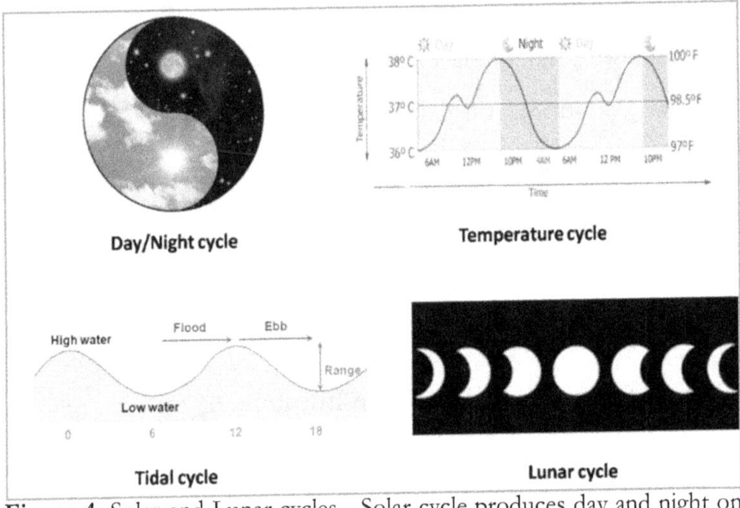

Figure 4: Solar and Lunar cycles - Solar cycle produces day and night on earth in predictable manner which in turn produces rhythmicity in temperature on earth. Lunar cycle is observed in the form of moon phases which gives rise to tidal cycles on earth.

Human behavior is dominated by geophysical sunrise and sunset. The increasing isolation of the human societies from the geophysical cycles, have led many to believe that human biology functions independently of them. Although the seasonal and daily rhythms have been fairly well described, little is known about the effects of the lunar cycle on the behavior and physiology of humans. Lunar cycles had and continue to have an influence on human culture, though despite a persistent belief that our mental health and other behaviors are modulated by the phase of the moon, there is no scientific evidence that human psychology is in any way regulated by the lunar cycle.

The belief that the moon can have an effect on human physiology and especially reproductive activity is usually justified on the basis that the human body contains 80% water and that the moon exerts its influence, like the tides due to its gravity. The gravitational forces which generate the tides depend upon the distance between the earth and the moon and on the alignment of the moon, earth and sun and not on phases of the moon. Gravity is a remarkably weak force. Whilst the moon clearly influences oceanic tides, it does not produce tides in smaller bodies of water such as lakes and even some seas.

Human biology is also dependent upon the 24 h revolution of the earth upon its axis. Earth is tilted to 23.5^0 to its axis which causes various seasons on the earth. Oceans cover 71% of earth's surface. Because of its fluid nature, this great body of water within confluent basins is easily deformed by the lunar gravitational pulls. The dramatic tidal, semilunar and lunar cyclic changes in water level that result from the moon's influence profoundly affect the lives of many marine organisms.

Effect of geophysical cycles on other animals

Many marine organisms were studied for their response to tidal and lunar cycles. The Palolo worm (*Eunice viridis*) is found on several coral islands near Samoa and the Fiji islands. The Palolos reproduce by swarming during the last quarter of the moon in October and November. The terminal parts of their bodies drop off and float over the surface of the water, releasing sperm and eggs. The natives of the Samoan islands have known this for centuries and predict the day and time of the day when the emergence occurs so that they can be ready to catch worms for food. Studies have attempted to determine whether it is the direct effect of lunar illuminance which stimulates swarming.

Some animals are clearly influenced by the moon and possess internal clocks which are dependent on the lunar cycle. Many organisms living in tidal zones use the lunar cycle to anticipate tides. The orbital motions of the earth, moon and sun and their gravitational and centrifugal forces generate the tides. As a result, life in the intertidal zone experiences a 12.8 hour rise and fall of the water level. In addition to these gravitational forces, many nocturnal species and species that sleep in the open are also exposed to marked changes in the brightness of the light reflected from the lunar surface every lunar month (a period of 29.53 days).

At full moon, the illuminance is approximately 25 times greater than at the quarter moon and 250 times greater than a moonless clear night sky. In response to these predictive events in the environment, numerous species have evolved endogenous clocks to anticipate these tidal, semilunar and lunar cycles.

Seasonal rhythms

With some exceptions, non-equatorial animals do not breed all year round. They save energy by effectively 'turning off' their reproductive organs for much of the year. In many species, the gonads regress and in some they almost vanish. In the non-breeding state, the reproductive organs of many seasonal birds weigh no more than 0.2% of body weight. But in full breeding condition the testes of the male birds can weigh between 1-2% of total body weight.

Many animals also show seasonal patterns of migration and hibernation, underpinned by profound changes in their physiology and behavior. The seasonal change in day-length, temperature and the consequent availability of food dominates the lives of most non-equatorial species. Animal studies reveal that the lunar cycle may affect hormonal changes early in phylogenesis (eg. insects). In fish, the lunar clock influences reproduction and involves the hypothalamic-pituitary-gonadal glands. In birds, the daily variations in melatonin and corticosterone disappear during full moon days. The lunar cycle also exerts effects on laboratory rats, with regards to taste sensitivity and the ultrastructure of pineal gland cells. The release of neurohormones may be triggered by the gravitational pull of the moon. A study conducted on honeybees showed a 29.5 day rhythm regarding triacylglycerols and steroids in the hemolymph as well as body weight peaking at the new moon.

Studies on fish demonstrated that fish physiology is influenced by lunar periodicity and correlates with hormonal changes. A study on golden rabbit fish, *Siganus guttatus* which spawns synchronously around the first quarter moon during the reproductive season, showed daily fluctuations of melatonin concentration in the blood, which was low during the day and high at night.

Reports on effects of the lunar cycle on the physiology of amphibians and reptiles are lacking. Amphibians and reptiles are subject to seasonal changes due to hibernation in winter. In the night migrating skylark, *Alauda arvensis* the main nocturnal movements take place during the waxing phase of the moon. A direct effect of lunar light may have significance in the fluctuation of physical processes in free-living animals. It is unlikely that laboratory animals kept in an isolated place with a light-dark cycle of 12 hours each could also be subject to such effects.

It is also likely that laboratory animal which does not perceive lunar light, in contrast to free living animals, have elevated concentration of melatonin during full moon days. There are indications that the cyclic moon initiates neurohormonal activity in the hypothalamus and the pituitary gland. Surprisingly, however, moon-induced cyclic changes in the steroid levels can also be observed in the honey bee, whose nervous system is much less complex. These examples are indicative of the effect of exogenous rhythmic phenomena on the biology of animals.

Effect of geophysical cycles on plants

Just as the moon influences the rise and fall of the tides, it also has a gravitational effect on the moisture in plants (sap), the soil and water table. As the moon light increases (new moon and second quarter), this stimulates leaf growth of plants. After the full moon, the moon light decreases, putting energy in the plant roots. At this time, the above-ground leaf growth slows down.

The study carried out to measure the effect of lunar cycle on the growth of Ashwagandha (*Withania somnifera*) plant. It is assessed by the parameters such as root weight, pith diameter and inter-nodal distance which found to be increased on full moon days as compared to new moon days. In the leguminous plants soyabean, peanut and clover "sleep movements" change the position of leaves from horizontal during the day to vertical at night.

Summary

- Daily rising and setting of the moon, along with the monthly waxing and waning cycles have effects on oceans and seas.

- There is no sufficient experimental evidence that the moon affects human mental and physical health, though the effect has been observed in other organisms.

- Human biology is also dependent upon the 24 h revolution of the earth upon its axis. Earth is tilted to 23.5^0 to its axis which causes various seasons on the earth.

- For many animals, particularly birds, the moon is essential for migration and navigation; while other animals time their reproduction to coincide with the specific phases of the lunar cycle.

- For marine invertebrate animals, rhythmic pattern of locomotor, reproductive and molting behavior is regulated by lunar and semilunar periodicity.

- The amount of moonlight at different times influences the growth of plants.

Exercise

A] Multiple choice questions:

1. Moon produces tides in __________.

    a. Smaller water bodies
    b. Oceans
    c. Lakes

2. Palalo worms reproduce by swarming during the ______ quarter of moon

    a. First
    b. Second
    c. Last

3. In birds, the daily variation in melatonin and corticosterone disappear during _____ days.

    a. Full moon
    b. New Moon
    c. Sunny days

4. In the night migrating skylark the main nocturnal movements take place during the _________ phase of the moon.

   a. Waxing

   b. Waning

   c. No

5. Growth of the *Ashwagandha* plant has found to be increased on _______ day.

   a. New moon

   b. Airy

   c. Full moon

B] Answer the following:

1. There is no consistent association with the moon and human pathology, physiology of behavior – Explain.

2. Giving two examples explain how animals are influenced by moon.

3. State the effect of geophysical cycles on plants.

C] Activities:

Biological Rhythms in plant

1. Observe the sleep movements of plants in relation to light. Plot the graph of angle made by the leaves to the stem at various selected time points of the day and night for 24 hrs. You may select either *Mimosa pudica* or *Oxalis* plant.

2. Cell size variation over time - Observe under microscope the size of the cell of *Allium cepa* (onion) at various selected time points of the day and night. Plot the graph of cell size vs time.

Glossary

Circalunar rhythms:

Rhythms with a period of about 30 ±5 days (eg. menstrual cycle in adult women)

Circannual rhythms:

Oscillate with a period of approximately one year (± 2 months), synchronized or unsynchronized with the calendar year.

Circatidal rhythms:

Having a period length of about one tidal cycle, usually 12.4 hours

Diurnal:

Referring to rhythmic behavior or process that peaks in the day time rather than at night

Endogenous rhythms:

Endogenous rhythms are independently oscillating systems that are able to maintain their periodicity.

References

- S. D. Tavhare, K. Nishteswar, and V. J. Shukla, "Influence of lunar cycles on growth of Ashwagandha (*Withania somnifera* [L.] Dunal)," (in eng), Ayu, vol. 36, no. 3, pp. 258-64, 2015 Jul-Sep 2015, doi: 10.4103/0974-8520.182763.

- Chronobiology: Biological Timing edited by Dunlap, Loros and DeCoursey. Sinauer associates Inc. 2004.

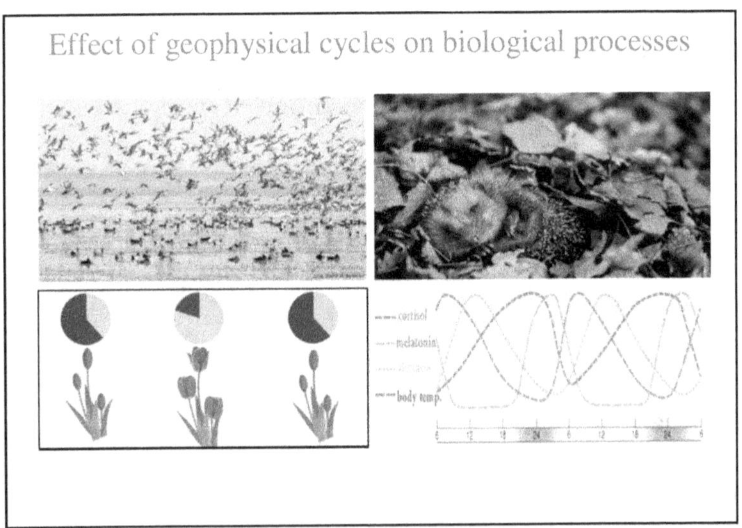

4 BIOLOGICAL RHYTHMS

Introduction

The cycle of day and night is one of the most dramatic features of the world in which we live. Because of this day and night cycle, almost all the species in the world exhibit daily changes in their behavior and physiology. These daily rhythms arise from a timekeeping system within the organism. This timekeeping system allows the organism to anticipate and prepare for the changes in the physical environment. Every organism has an inherent biological clock which is expressed in the form of rhythms.

Living entities have their own internal schedules. Biological clocks as they exist now may have evolved as a tool primarily adaptive to daily cycles of the natural environment. Initially several geophysical cycles may have played crucial roles in exerting selection pressure, while later, daily and seasonal changes may have further fine-tuned them. Biological processes were inherently rhythmic from the very first cell, that is, from the beginning of life itself. If life is fundamentally rhythmic, then our understanding of all fields of biology will be improved by studying the complex rhythmicity.

Biological rhythms are everywhere. They are exhibited by all eukaryotes and by at least one group of prokaryotes - the *Cyanobacteria*. All levels of biological organization such as ecosystem, population, group, individual, organ system, organ, tissue, cell and subcellular structure exhibit rhythms with diverse frequencies. Organisms cannot adjust immediately to new environmental schedules because biological rhythm includes complex internal timing systems.

Types of rhythms

Biological rhythms are classified by various criteria such as, descriptive or physiological or structural classification to name few. But the most prominent is the physical classification which is based on the length of the period of oscillation. Biological rhythms exhibit periods ranging from seconds, hours, days, weeks, months and even years as shown in figure 5. Though rhythms have very different periods, they are found to affect one another in subtle ways. Some of the examples of biological rhythms are tabulated below.

Table 2: Rhythmicity in nature and living systems

Rhythmic behavior in nature	Rhythmic behavior in living systems	Rhythmic behavior in humans
Day / Night cycle	Migration	Sleep / Wake cycle
Lunar cycle	Hibernation / Aestivation	Feeding cycle
Tidal cycle	Reproductive cycle	Bowel movement
Temperature cycle	Insect diapauses	Heart beat
Seasonal cycle	Germination / Flowering	Hormone release
Cyclones	Leaf/Stomatal movement	Menstrual cycle
Monsoon	Foraging courtship)	Nasal cycle

The rhythms whose period of oscillation is 24 +/- 4 hours are defined as 'circadian' (from circa diem, i.e., approximately one day). The cyclic events with a period of less than 20 hours or more than 28 hours are defined respectively as 'ultradian' and 'infradian'.

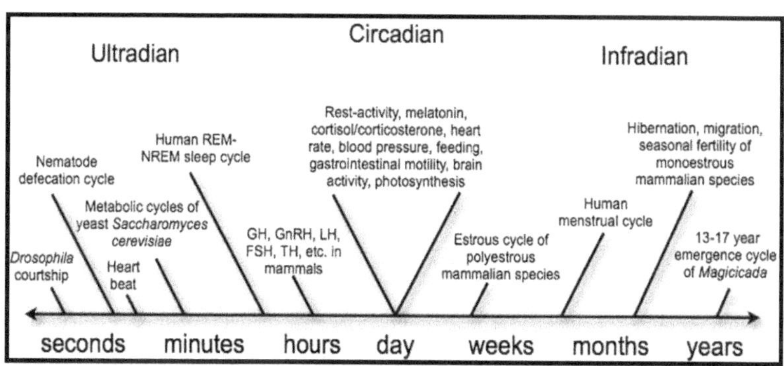

Figure 5: Types of rhythms – Ultradian, Circadian and Infradian classified based on period. (Adapted from Circadian and Ultradian Clocks/Rhythms-EW Lamont et al., 2017)

Ultradian Rhythm - These are biological rhythms that are shorter than 24 h. These rhythms have multiple cycles in one day. Ultradian rhythms regulate physical, emotional and psychological functions. Not much is known about the mechanism of initiation and regulation of ultradian rhythms which fine tunes all other types of biological rhythms. It was hypothesized that pacemaker for ultradian rhythm is present in Peri-Ventricular Nuclei (PVN) of hypothalamus in the brain.

There are many physiological functions of the human body that exemplify the ultradian rhythm. For example, an adult has an activity and rest cycle about every 2 h, nasal cycle of 4 h or the growth hormone production cycle of 3 h. Ultradian rhythms often last several hours and include the ingestion of food, circulation of blood, secretion of hormones. Some last merely for seconds, such as control of breathing. Some last for only milliseconds, such as the majority of processes that take place in the cell on a microcirculatory level. In nature, tidal rhythms are often observed in marine life which are of ultradian in nature.

In yeast, an ultradian rhythm of 40 min for cellular respiration is observed. Ultradian leaf movements of plants cover a range of periods from minutes (eg. *Desmodium gyransto*) to several hours (eg. *Phaseolus vulgaris*). Not only leaf movements but other physiological and chemical systems show oscillations in the ultradian period range. Hypocotyl circumnutations with period lengths ranging from 25 min to 8h are part of the process of stem elongation in *Arabidopsis*.

Circadian Rhythm – These are the most studied and well characterized biological rhythms with a period of about a day which will be discussed in more details later in the chapter.

Infradian rhythm -These are rhythms that last more than 24 hours. Infradian rhythm exhibits a frequency lower than that of the circadian rhythm. These are long term cycles which are repeated only every few days, weeks, months or even once per year such as the annual migration or reproduction cycles found in certain animals or the human menstrual cycle. Accordingly they may be described as circaseptan (weekly), circadiseptan (Biweekly), circatrigintan (monthly), or circannual (yearly).

For most of the true circannual species, photoperiod is the most important cue for synchronizing the rhythmic behavior. Non-photic synchronizers such as temperature, social stimuli, and food supplementation appear to have limited effect on circannual entrainment. Photoperiod is the length of the light phase in each daily (24 h) light–dark cycle which is also described by the ratio of light to darkness during a 24 h cycle. Photoperiodism is the biological process of responding to changes in photoperiod. Melatonin is an indole amine neurohormone that is produced and secreted nocturnally by the pineal gland, and is essential for seasonal photoperiodic responses in mammals. Although not the only parameter, the changing length of the photoperiod (day length) is the most predictive environmental cue for the seasonal timing of physiology and behaviour, most notably for timing of migration, hibernation and reproduction. Even though we are aware about the role of photoperiod and melatonin in generation of infradian rhythms, a dominant pacemaker site / organ which gives rise to the rhythm is yet to be identified in any of the organisms.

The phenomenon of photoperiodism is an excellent example of physiological preconditioning (or after-effect) where an external factor (i.e., the photoperiodic stimulus) induces some physiological changes in the plant, the effect of which is not immediately visible. Diapause, a period of dormancy in insects is often timed with photoperiod. Metabolic processes in ectothermic vertebrates are coupled to environmental temperature, thus annual rhythms are indirectly regulated by photoperiodism.

Circadian Rhythm

Circadian rhythms (from Latin 'Circa' meaning 'around' and 'diem' meaning day), a term coined by Franz Halberg which replaces earlier ambiguous terminologies, such as daily, diurnal, diel, 24 hour, or nycthemeral all meaning same. Circadian rhythms are the most prominent biological rhythms. Circadian rhythm consists of a periodic phenomenon in living organisms and their adaptation to solar and lunar related rhythms. A circadian rhythm is a roughly 24 h cycle in the physiological process of a living being including plants, animals, bacteria and cyanobacteria.

It can be said that the circadian rhythms are driven by the cycles of the environment as the period of a cycle in an organism often matches the period of an environmental cycle. Recent studies have highlighted the dominant role that circadian clock plays in the organization of the 24 h pattern of behavior and physiology. These rhythms are defined by major, observable and well established criteria and not by a molecular mechanism alone. Sleep-wake cycle, body temperature cycle are some of the examples of circadian rhythm. Circadian rhythms exist in all types of organisms. For example they help flowers open and close at the right and keep nocturnal animals from leaving their shelters during the day time when they would be exposed to more predators.

Melatonin

Melatonin, also known as the "mother hormone of chronobiology" is a hormone primarily released by the pineal gland at night, and has long been associated with control of the sleep-wake cycle. It controls our internal clock, stimulates the activity of numerous cell groups and regulates our sleep.

Melatonin has a short half-life of about 30 minutes. As it breaks down so quickly, it must be made continuously throughout the night in order to sustain restful sleep. Additionally this hormone has an antioxidant effect. If melatonin production is disturbed, or if not enough of the hormone is being produced or distributed at the right time, then our sleep is impaired, which can lead to a number of different illnesses.

Chemical formula of Melatonin - $C_{13}H_{16}N_2O_2$

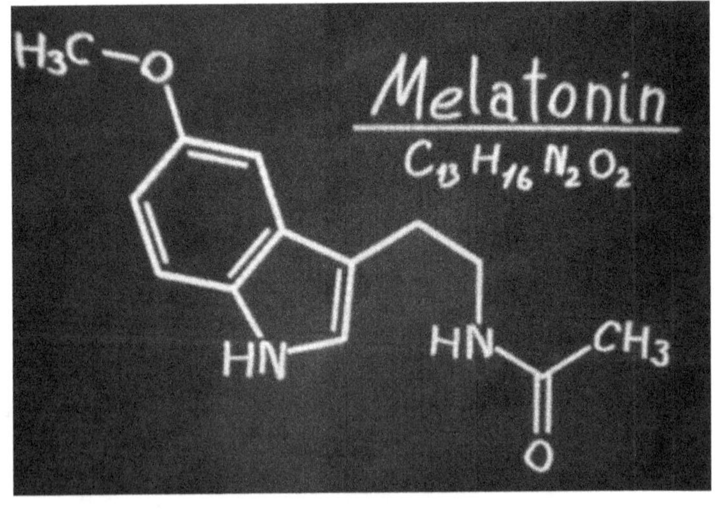

In humans, circadian rhythms in the body are synchronized to the environment by a master clock or pacemaker that is located in the suprachiasmatic nuclei (SCN). The SCN is a tiny region of the brain in the hypothalamus situated directly above the optic chiasma. The SCN receives information about light and darkness through a pigment called melanopsin present in retinal cells of the eyes, integrates this input and relays it to cellular circadian clocks located throughout the rest of the body.

In this way, circadian rhythms in behavior and physiology are synchronized to the external light-dark cycle. The central biological clock located in SCN further regulates peripheral clocks present in various organs in the body thus coordinating physiological processes throughout the day.

Properties of circadian rhythm

1. Endogenous rhythmicity: Circadian rhythms are endogenous in nature that regulate the timing of numerous physiological functions, although they can be modulated by external cues such as sunlight and temperature. Circadian rhythm persists even in the absence of environmental cues such as day and night cycle and maintains its periodicity close to 24 h. It is interesting to note that totally blind subterranean mammals, for example, blind mole rats are able to maintain their endogenous clocks in the apparent absence of external stimuli.

2. Temperature compensation: The second key property is that the circadian rhythms are temperature compensated. This means that a 24 h rhythm does not speed up or slow down very much, even when the external temperature might change greatly. The temperature compensatory behavior of circadian clocks was demonstrated by Pittendrigh (1954). Temperature compensation allows organisms to maintain robust rhythms over a broad range of physiological temperatures. The influence of temperature on circadian rhythm is interesting, in that a change in temperature can affect the phase of the cycle without substantially altering the rate of cycling. This means that the cycle may start at earlier or later than normal time but still have the same length.

3. Ubiquity: Circadian rhythms exist in a broad array of biological processes and organisms, with similar properties and even similar phase-response curves to light. The Phase Response Curve (PRC) is a curve describing the relationship between a stimulus, such as light exposure, and a response illustrated in diagram below. Circadian rhythms appear to be evolutionarily conserved from unicellular organisms to highly complex mammals.

4. Entrainment: The rhythm can be reset by exposure to external stimuli (such as light, heat or food). The process of adjustment is called entrainment. Travel across time zones illustrates the ability of the human biological clock to adjust the local time; a person will usually experience jet lag before entrainment of their circadian clock has brought it into synchronization with local time. The exogenous/ external factors that entrain the endogenous rhythms are called zeitgebers or entraining factors. Since strong zeitgeber defines the rhythm of the clockwork, time is expressed as zeitgeber time (ZT).

5. Free run: Circadian rhythms that are expressed in the absence of any 24 h signals from the external environment are called free running. This means that the endogenous rhythm is not synchronized to any cyclic change in the physical environment. The free-running rhythms, therefore, may be transformed into synchronized rhythms, and the endpoint of this interplay is a 'masking effect' exerted by the exogenous component on the endogenous bio periodicity.

In nature, the overt manifestation for most biological rhythms is the combination of the endogenous component plus the exogenous entrainment. In this case, the masking effect results in a synchronized rhythm, and the external factors of masking can be defined as 'entraining agents' or 'zeitgebers' or 'synchronizers'. The period length of these free-running rhythms is often no longer equal to 24 hours and differs from species to species. Therefore, time cannot be expressed in ZT but is expressed in circadian time (CT) units.

Thus an organism's circadian clock is defined as an endogenous and temperature compensated mechanism, which counts a day as occurring over the length of the free running period, but which is normally susceptible to entrainment for the local 24 h cycle. which is normally susceptible to entrainment to the local 24 hour cycle.

Is circadian rhythm the same as a biological clock?

Not all biological clocks are circadian. Circadian rhythm is an effect of a biological clock.

Biological clocks help regulate the timing of biological processes including circadian rhythms. For instance, plants adjust changing seasons using a biological clock with timing distinct from a 24-hour cycle.

Representation of a rhythm

Each biological rhythm is composed of repeating units called cycles. A representative biological rhythm is depicted in which the level of a particular measure (for example, blood hormone levels and activity level) varies according to time. The biological rhythm is a cyclic phenomenon defined by four parameters - period, phase, amplitude and mean as shown in Figure 6A.

Period - Period is the necessary time for the cycle to be completed, measured as the time between two consecutive maximum (peaks) or minimal (troughs) periods.

Phase - The phase is defined as any point in the cycle that is known for its relation to the rest of the cycle. In other words, any specified recognizable part of a cycle is called phase. The most obvious phase points are the peak and trough positions.

Amplitude - The magnitude of the change in activity rate during a cycle is called the amplitude. Thus, amplitude is considered as the distance between the peak (or trough) and mean value of the wave. The amplitude of a biological rhythm may often vary, while the period remains unchanged.

Mean/MESOR - A measure of central tendency of the distribution of instantaneous values of an oscillating variable. The mesor (acronym for **M**idline **E**stimating **S**tatistic **of** **R**hythm) is a circadian rhythm-adjusted mean.

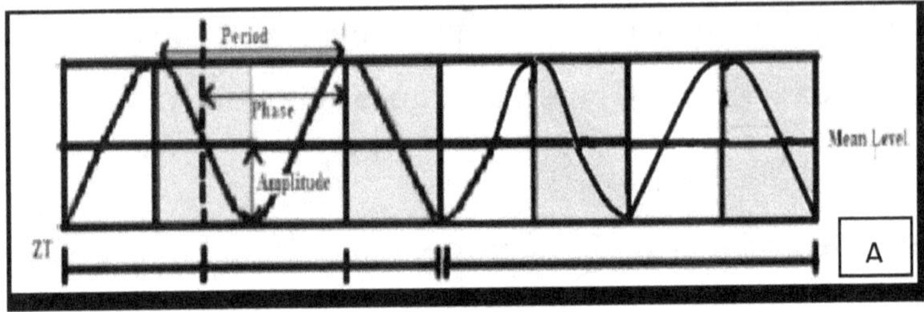

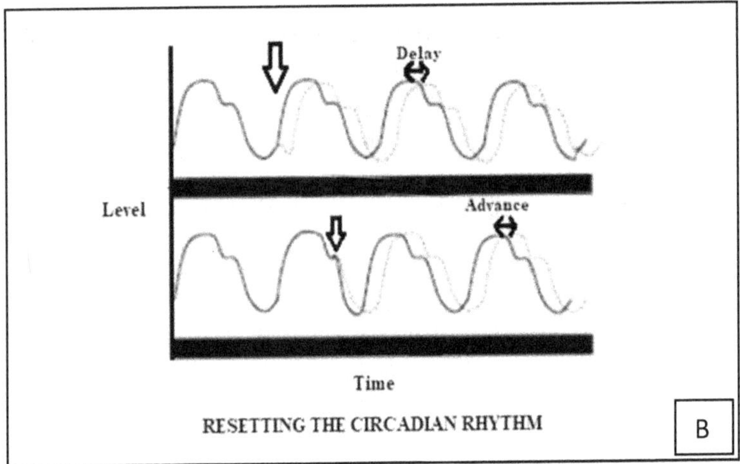

Figure 6: A) Characteristics of circadian rhythm – A typical rhythm is characterized by period, amplitude, phase and mean level. B) Resetting of circadian rhythm – A rhythm can be entrained by external cues such as light, food or activity which is represented by phase advance or phase delay.

Representation of entrainment of the rhythm

The time difference between the entraining external and the displayed internal rhythm (e.g. the onset of an animal's activity) is called phase angle difference (Ψ).

A phase shift (ϕ) is defined as the resetting of the organism's internal rhythm in response to an external stimulus such as nocturnal light exposure. Such a phase shift can either result in a phase advance or a phase delay as shown in figure 6B.

Summary

- Biological rhythms are the natural cycle of changes in our body's function. .

- There are three biological rhythms based on difference in period length. Ultradian rhythms are rhythms that occur more frequently than 24 hours. Circadian rhythms are daily rhythms that are approximately 24 hours. Infradian rhythms are rhythms that are longer than 24 hours.

- Circadian rhythm is an endogenous biological rhythm. It is temperature compensated, that is, it maintains the same period over a wide range of temperatures.

- The biological rhythms are entrainable. Light and food are major entraining agents.

- Four main parameters of biological rhythms are period, phase, amplitude and mean.

Exercise

A] Multiple Choice Questions:

1. Every organism has an inherent _________ clock which is expressed by rhythms.

    a. Biological

    b. External

    c. Glass sand

2. Ultradian rhythms have ________ in one day.

    a. One cycle

    b. No cycle

    c. Multiple cycles

3. ________ is an example of circadian rhythm.

    a. Tidal rhythm

    b. Sleep-wake cycle

    c. Annual migration of birds

4. Circadian rhythms are ________

    a. Entrainable

    b. Endogenous

    c. Both (a) and (b)

5. ________ is the necessary time for the cycle to be completed as the time between two consecutive peaks and troughs.

    a. Amplitude

    b. Period

    c. Phase

B] Answer the following:

1. What is the biological rhythm? Give its types.

2. Distinguish between ultradian rhythm and infradian rhythm.

3. What are the characteristic properties of circadian rhythm?

4. Write a note on representation of rhythm.

C] Activity:

1. Twinning cycle in plant: Experiment and examine the twinning movements of the Bean plant's growing tip. Observe the movement of the shoot Period of the twinning cycle.

2. Eclosion rhythm in fruit fly: Maintain the culture of fruit fly with standard protocol. Observe and note down the eclosion pattern during the development of fruit fly.

3. Effect of antibiotics on bacterial growth: Observe the effect of antibiotics on bacterial growth of *E.coli* / *S.aureus* during selective time points of the day.

Glossary

Amplitude:

The extent of an oscillatory movement, measured from mean to extreme value.

Circadian Time (CT):

a. Subjective internal organism time in which one circadian period is divided into 24 equal parts each a circadian hour. By convention, CT0 corresponds to subjective dawn and CT12 to subjective dusk.

b. The quantification of time as defined by an organism's circadian clock, without reference to any environmental regularities or zeitgebers.

Entrainment:

a. Coupling of two rhythms of the same frequency to one of them (the entraining agent or synchronizer) determining the phase of the other. It is coupling of endogenous rhythms to the environmental oscillator of the same frequency or determination of the phase of biological rhythms by an internal pacemaker.

b. The process whereby circadian clocks actively synchronize to cyclic environmental signals (zeitgeber: predominantly light and dark)

c. The process by which an environmental rhythm such as day-night cycle regulates the period and phase relationship of self-sustained biological pacemakers.

Free run:

a. An organism that is in constant conditions (LL or DD) and not exposed to any exogenous time cues.

b. Circadian clocks can produce self-sustained rhythms even in the constant environment (i.e. without zeitgeber signals) under such conditions their rhythms run free.

c. The state of an oscillator when not influenced by any external time cues.

Free Running Period (FRP):

The period length of a biological oscillator which corresponds to the length of time it takes for an organism's endogenous rhythm to repeat (return to the same phase) in the absence of environmental time cue.

Period:

The time after which a defined phase of an oscillator recurs which generally refers to the amount of time it takes a cyclic process to return to the same phase.

Phase:

The instantaneous state of an oscillation within a period.

Phase response curve:

a. A map of phase dependent resetting that is the phase dependent response to a circadian clock to an entraining agent delivered at different times through a circadian day.

b. A graph representing the varying effect that an identical stimulus has on circadian rhythms phase, depending on the phase of circadian time at which it is applied.

Phase shift:

a. The steady state change in phase brought about by the action of an entraining agent.

b. A change (either advance or a delay) in the phasing of an organism's free running circadian rhythm, usually in response to an acute stimulus.

Periodicity:

A system or process exhibits periodicity if it has a tendency to repeat some process at a constant interval (that is, with some well-defined period.

Spontaneous desynchronization:

The phenomenon in which two oscillators that had been mutually entrained spontaneously move out of phase with one another.

Subjective Day:

a. The portion of a circadian day in a constant darkness corresponding to the day phase in a light-dark cycle.

b. The phase of daylight as predicted by the organism's endogenous clock in the absence of zeitgebers; anchored to onset of activity in nocturnal organisms, but not in diurnal organisms.

Subjective Night:

a. The portion of a circadian day in a constant darkness corresponding to the night phase in a light-dark cycle.

b. The phase of night as predicted by the organism's endogenous clock in the absence of zeitgebers; anchored to onset of activity in nocturnal organisms, but not in diurnal organisms.

Synchronizer:

a. An agent that promotes synchrony between or among oscillators.

b. The environmental periodicity determining the temporal placement of a biological rhythm along an appropriate time scale.

Synchronization:

The state of a system when two or more variables exhibit periodicity with the same frequency. It refers to the adjustment of endogenous rhythm to external periodic influences.

Temperature compensation:

The ability of the circadian clock to maintain a relatively constant free running period despite fluctuations in environmental temperature.

Zeitgeber:

From the German 'time giver' or 'synchronizer', it is an external time cue or cyclic environmental signals that are effective in entraining an organism, for example, light dark, regular feeding.

Zeitgeber Time (ZT):

A quantification of time, defined with reference to environmental regularities or zeitgebers.

References

- D. A. Paranjpe and V. K. Sharma, "Evolution of temporal order in living organisms," (in eng), J Circadian Rhythms, vol. 3, no. 1, p. 7, May 2005, doi: 10.1186/1740-3391-3-7.

- B. G. B. Solheim, A. Johnsson, and T. H. Iversen, "Ultradian rhythms in Arabidopsis thaliana leaves in microgravity," (in eng), New Phytol, vol. 183, no. 4, pp. 1043-1052, 2009, doi: 10.1111/j.1469-8137.2009.02896.x.

- D. E. Somers, "The physiology and molecular bases of the plant circadian clock," (in eng), Plant Physiol, vol. 121, no. 1, pp. 9-20, Sep 1999, doi: 10.1104/pp.121.1.9.

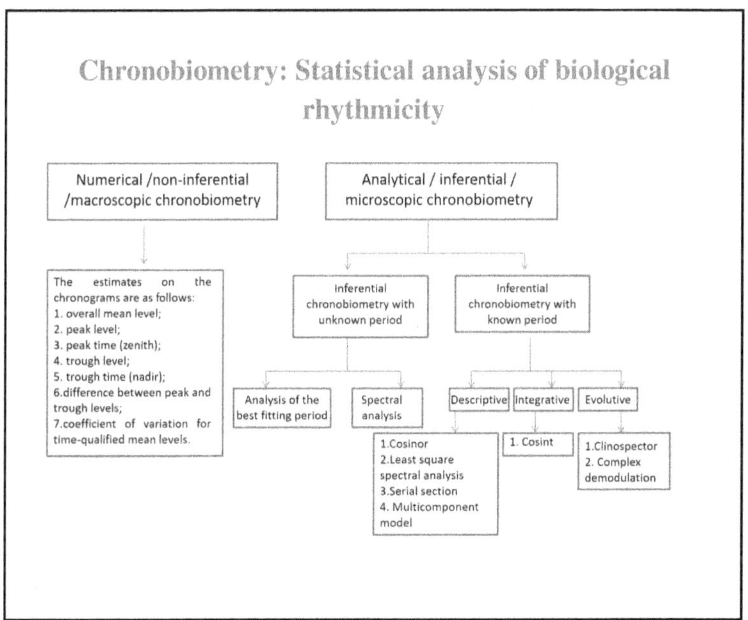

HOME | HISTORY OF THE SYMPOSIA | LIST OF SYMPOSIA | USE OF IMAGES

Biological Clocks

1960

Symposium Synopsis

Organizer: Arthur Chovnick

While daily rhythms have been studied systematically for many years, there has been a most remarkable outburst of interest in the subject during the past ten years. This growth of interest is due, almost entirely, to the elegant experimental demonstrations that birds, bees, and many other animals orient or "navigate" using the position of the sun as a guidepost, and compensating for its movement in time with the use of an internal chronometer. Rapid advances have been seen in studies of rather diverse phenomena in a wide variety of organisms from single cells through higher plants and animals.

By bringing together leading investigators from throughout the world who are intimately concerned with the broad array of phenomena classified under the general topic "Biological Clocks", it is hoped that this year's Symposium may serve as a unifying influence on the entire field of study.

The program this year was organized by a committee consisting of C. S. Pittendrigh (Chairman), J. Aschoff, V. G. Bruce, E. Bunning, D. R. Griffin, and J. W. Hastings. Serving as chairmen of the program sessions were: C. S. Pittendrigh, E. BunningvJ Aschoff, S. B. Hendricks, V. G. Bruce, H. Kalmus, O. H. Schmitt, A. D. Lees, K. V. Thimann, C. P. Richter, F. Halberg, R. Bunsow, D. R. Griffin, K. S. Rawson, K. Hoffmann, A. D. Hasler, and F. A. Brown, Jr. The Laboratory is indeed grateful to all of these gentlemen for their efforts in organizing and conducting the program.

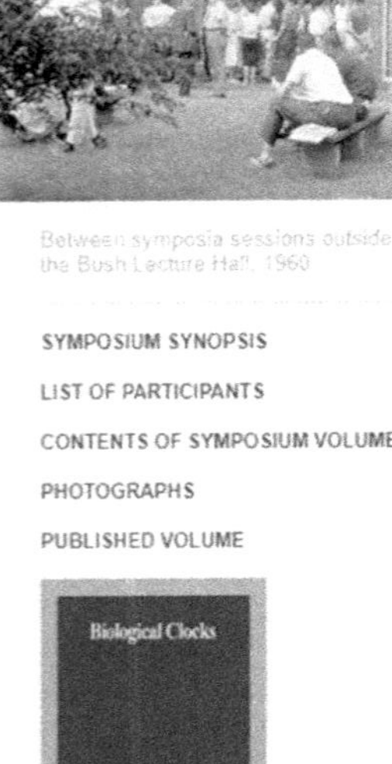

SYMPOSIUM SYNOPSIS

LIST OF PARTICIPANTS

CONTENTS OF SYMPOSIUM VOLUME

PHOTOGRAPHS

PUBLISHED VOLUME

PART II

STRUCTURAL AND FUNCTIONAL EVOLUTION OF CLOCK SYSTEM

5 STRUCTURAL COMPONENTS AND ANATOMICAL ORGANIZATION OF INTERNAL CLOCK

Introduction

Daily rhythms in biochemical, cellular and behavioral activities are controlled by the biological clock which consists of one or more endogenous oscillators. Although circadian rhythms are present in different organisms, several aspects of clock mechanism and its complexity are not conserved among them. In circadian rhythm, oscillations with approximately 24 h periods in many physiological activities, are found in a wide spectrum of organisms. These periodic rhythms result from a complex interplay among clock components that are specific to organisms. A full understanding of these processes requires a detailed knowledge of clockwork components.

Circadian Clock

The basic structure of many circadian systems is composed of a central oscillator located within the cell which controls output pathways that drive the observable rhythms. The phase of the oscillation is set by an input pathway that responds to external time cues. Circadian clock consists of multiple oscillators wherein the pacemaker is the central oscillator that entrains to the external environmental cues and regulates the rhythm output directly and/or by synchronizing slave oscillators which then regulate given output. The slave oscillators are entrained by the central oscillator. Multiple oscillators have been observed in *Cyanobacteria* and *Neurospora*. Unicellular organisms and plants lack organ level organization of circadian rhythmicity. In case of multicellular organisms, the basic circadian system is believed to consist of at least three important components as shown in figure 7.

1. Photoreceptor

2. Pacemaker or Oscillator

3. Outputs

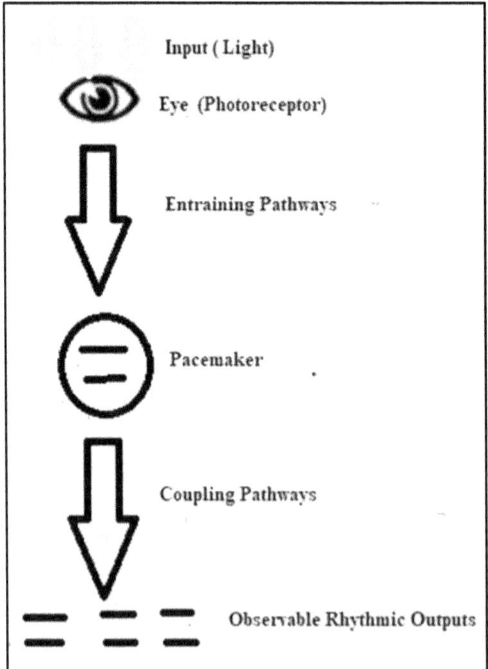

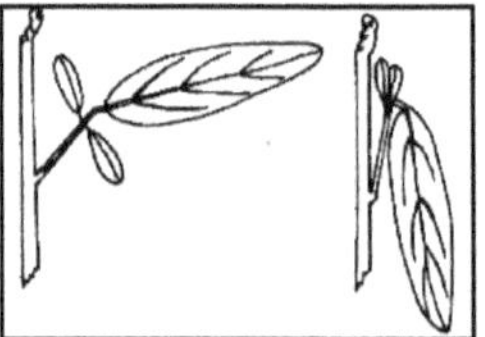

Figure 7: Basic components of circadian system: A) Higher organisms except plants exhibit organ level organization circadian system in the form of photoreceptor, pacemaker and observable output mechanisms. B) Plants have decentralized circadian system with leaf movement as prominent rhythmic output.

1. Photoreceptor:

The circadian rhythm clocks are synchronized to the periodic environmental changes like day/night cycles, by specific stimuli. Among these, the most important is the light.

In most of the animals it was found that the eyes possess the primary receptors. They (except mammals) also have an ability to perceive extra optic light signals.

In plants, photoreceptors, phytochromes and cryptochromes are involved in setting the clock by transducing the light signal to the central oscillator.

2. Pacemaker:

Pacemakers are the oscillators which generate biological rhythms in the absence of external periodic inputs.

Central circadian pacemakers that control animal behavior are located in the brains of insects and rodents but the location of such a pacemaker has not been determined in plants. Higher plants contain a spatial array of autonomous circadian clocks that regulate gene expression without a biological pacemaker. The hypothalamic suprachiasmatic nuclei are the dominant pacemaker of many circadian rhythms in mammals.

3. Output:

Circadian output comprises the business end of circadian systems in terms of adaptive significance.

The utilitarian and therefore the most important aspect of all clocks, often referred to as output, is the ability to invoke "time of dayness" onto the organism, such that it can predict daily changes in the environment to regulate its own changing metabolic needs over the course of the diurnal cycle. Most outputs may occur in a linear fashion and be distinct from the clock mechanism.

Accordingly, different models have been given by scientists to explain the working of the circadian oscillator. For example, in the Chronon model, the 24 hour period is ascribed to the time taken for the transcription of a hypothetical linear sequence of DNA, cistron by cistron. According to the membrane model, the period is attributed to the slower process involved in the lateral fusion of proteins with the lipid layer. According to yet another model, the circadian period is believed to be the result of interactions between higher frequency biochemical oscillations within the cell.

Circadian rhythm is not exclusive to human beings. Almost every living organism, microorganisms to plants and animals, in other words from single cell to multicellular species has its own circadian rhythm. Various invertebrate model systems such as molluscs and insects have been employed to understand structural components of circadian clocks.

Circadian clock in plants

Internal timekeeper i.e. circadian clock in plants anticipates environmental cues such as light, temperature and regulates photoperiodic rhythmicity for the proper growth and fitness of the plant. The plants showing circadian rhythm have biological clocks inside their cells which measure the passage of time. The nature and functioning of biological clocks is not yet clearly understood. The location of the biological clock too is not clear in the cells because circadian rhythms are not observed in cell free extracts or isolated cell organelles. It is likely that the biological clock does not lie within the cell but the whole cell itself probably acts as the biological clock.

Plants lack multicellular circadian pacemakers, even though they have many circadian regulatory processes, as well as circadian photoreceptors scattered in their leaves. Each plant cell is thought to have its own circadian oscillator that can operate independently, but recent research has found that there is communication between the circadian oscillators of different tissue types.

> ## How do researchers study circadian rhythms?
>
> Scientists learn about circadian rhythms by studying humans and by using organisms with similar biological clocks genes like fruit flies and mice. While doing various experiments, researchers control the subjects' environment by alternating light and dark periods. Then the changes in gene activity or other molecular signals are observed.
>
> Researchers also observe the organisms with regular circadian rhythms and identify which genetic components of biological clocks may be broken. Understanding more about the genes responsible for circadian rhythms will help us to know more about the human body.

Circadian clock in unicellular organisms

A cell-autonomous circadian oscillatory mechanism has been known for many years to be the source of endogenous circadian rhythmicity in unicellular organisms. In unicellular organisms, mounting evidence indicates the existence of more than one oscillator within a single cell, each of which is predicted to consist of different components.

Single cells are valuable circadian models as they cast considerable light on circadian rhythms of higher organisms. Additionally, unicellular organisms are a more uniform substrate for biochemical analysis than complex multicellular organisms. For example in marine flagellate *Gonyaulax polyedra*, two oscillators that respond to different wavelengths of light are thought to differentially regulate the rhythms of bioluminescence and phototaxis. These oscillators might include so-called 'slave-oscillators' that are normally synchronized by a pacemaker, or might themselves be pacemakers that function to regulate distinct outputs.

Model systems from unicellular organisms

- *Synechococcus* (prokaryotic *Cyanobacteria*)
- *Euglena* (eukaryotic euglenoids)
- *Paramecium* and *Tetrahymena* (eukaryotic ciliates)
- *Gonyaulax* (eukaryotic dinoflagellates)
- *Acetabularia* (eukaryotic chlorophytes)

Circadian clock in *Cyanobacteria*

Circadian clock in *Cyanobacteria* is cell autonomous. It is functionally different from eukaryotic oscillators because it is mainly based on post translational regulations. In cyanobacteria a biochemical oscillator acts as a pacemaker where three proteins form the core oscillator; KaiC. KaiA and KaiB. Their circadian rhythms are driven by a transcription and translation based autoregulatory loop of KaiBC gene expression, wherein KaiA and KaiC act respectively, as positive and negative regulators of KaiBC gene expression.

Circadian clock in *Neurospora*

Studies in *Neurospora crassa* have helped to understand many of the basic mechanisms that underlie circadian rhythms, including negative feedback and light and temperature entrainment, which are common to all clock systems. The *Neurospora crassa* clock controls several rhythmic processes, the most frequently assayed of which is the daily production of asexual conidiospores.

Cellular circadian clock of *Neurospora crassa* is a network composed of coupled circadian oscillators and at least one other autonomous circadian oscillator that responds differently to environmental inputs and can direct diverse outputs. The presence of several oscillators probably contributes to the diverse rhythmic processes that are under clock control. Thus in *Neurospora*, a core clock component directly provides an input pathway by integrating blue light information into the circadian system and guarantees the synchronization of the endogenous clock to the 24h day-night cycle.

Circadian clock in *Drosophila*

Almost all tissues show rhythmic clock gene expressions and therefore contain circadian oscillators. These oscillators are roughly divided into the 'central oscillator' which comprises several groups of neurons in the brain that control locomotory activity rhythms and 'Peripheral oscillators' which comprise of all other oscillators in the head and body. Circadian oscillators in isolated peripheral tissues like wings, legs and antennae function autonomously and are directly entrainable by light, which indicates that each oscillator might function as a pacemaker.

Thus the circadian clock in *Drosophila* shows two distinct groups, namely the clock neurons and clock genes. Clock genes act together with clock neurons to produce a 24 h cycle of rest and activity. Light is the source of activation of clocks. The compound eyes, ocelli and Hofbauer-Buchner eyelets (HB-eyelets) are the direct external photoreceptor organs. But the circadian clock can work in constant darkness. The compound eyes are important for differentiating long days from constant light. There are two distinct activity peaks, termed the M (morning) peak, happening at dawn and E (Evening) peak, at dusk. The light sensitive proteins in the eye, called rhodopsins are crucial in activating the M and E oscillations.

The clock neurons are located in distinct clusters in the central brain. The best understood cluster of neurons are the large and small lateral ventral neurons (l-LNvs and s-LNvs) of the optic lobes. s-LNvs receive light input from retinal photoreceptors in the compound eyes and extra-retinal photoreceptors within the brain; however they can also be entrained directly by light that penetrates the cuticle. In constant dark (DD) conditions, SLNvs maintain robust rhythms in gene expression and locomotor activity. These neurons produce pigment dispersing factor (PDF), a neuropeptide that acts as a circadian neuromodulator between different clock neurons. When environmental light is detected, approximately 150 neurons (there are about 100,000 neurons in the *Drosophila* brain) in the brain regulate the circadian rhythm.

There is much more diversity found in insect circadian systems. As cerebral lobes in fruit-fly act as pacemaker, it resides in optic lobes in case of cockroaches and beetles. In many other varieties of insects the pacemaker is even found outside the nervous system such as epidermal cells of cuticle, complex of testes and seminal ducts or ecdysone secreting prothoracic glands.

Circadian clock in Molluscs

Well-developed circadian rhythmicity is known for two molluscan species namely, *Alysia calfornica* - the sea hare and *Bulla gouldiana* - the clouded bubble snail. Both are marine gastropod molluscs. Both are behaviorally and structurally simple animals. Two simple eyes each of which contain a circadian pacemaker, are embedded in the body wall.

In both the animals, the eyes exhibit circadian rhythms of spontaneous nerve discharge activity that can easily be monitored within vitro preparations along the optic nerve. The circadian rhythm generated among approximately 100 neurons at the base of the retina referred to as basal retinal neurons. These basal retinal neurons intracellularly exhibits a circadian rhythm in membrane potential that appears to be driven by a circadian modulation of membrane conductance. Membrane conductance is relatively high during the subjective night and decreases after subjective dawn. Individual neurons can act as circadian pacemakers. The output of the ocular pacemaker to the central nervous system in both *Bulla* and *Aplysia* travels via the optic nerve.

Circadian clock in Birds

The avian circadian system constitutes pacemakers that regulate peripheral tissues that are present in the pineal gland, the retina and the SCN. In birds, SCN consists of two structures, visual SCN and medial SCN. The contribution of these pacemakers to the clock varies considerably among avian species.

A 'neuroendocrine-loop model' for avian circadian organization has been proposed to explain interactions between the components of the pacemaker in this complex system. The premise of this model is that the system is composed of circadian oscillators that reside within the SCN, the retina and the pineal gland. These oscillators are damped oscillators, in that the amplitude of the rhythm becomes reduced over time, but are capable of self-sustained oscillation in the presence of photic input and/or neural or endocrine input from the rest of the system.

A related model, the 'internal resonance model', proposed by Gwinner suggests that oscillator in the pineal and SCN stabilize and amplify each other through the secretion of periodic signal by both the SCN and pineal that is perceived by the other tissue (resonance).

In both the models, each pacemaker directly receives photic input: the pineal gland contains several photopigments and phototransduction systems that affect melatonin biosynthesis and the VSCN receives photic input from the retina through retinal hypothalamic tract (RHT). Each pacemaker in the avian circadian system might independently affect downstream processes.

The pineal gland influences the CNS and the peripheral sites through the secretion of melatonin during the night and tissues that express melatonin receptors are affected by these pacemakers directly. Coordination of avian circadian output through pacemakers in the pineal gland and the SCN might affect many physiological outputs.

Circadian clock in Mammals

The circadian system of mammals is composed of a hierarchy of oscillators that function at the cellular, tissue and system level. This system controls a wide variety of physiological functions, including sleep-wake cycles, body temperature, hormone secretion, locomotory activity and feeding behavior.

Circadian clocks are self - sustained; circadian oscillations that are intrinsic to each cell can occur autonomously without the need for an environmental signal. External cues reset the system daily and thereby prevent the endogenous clock from free running out of phase. The predominant external cue of the central clock is light.

In mammals, the anatomical structure in the brain that governs circadian rhythms is a small area consisting of ~ 15,000 neurons localized in the anterior hypothalamus, called the suprachiasmatic nucleus (SCN). This 'central pacemaker' receives signals from the environment and coordinates the oscillating activity of peripheral clocks, which are located in almost all tissues. Specialized cells in the retina detect the light signal that is then transmitted to the SCN via the retino-hypothalamic tract (RHT). At the level of SCN neurons, the light signal stimulates a cascade of signaling pathways that lead to the activation of a transcriptional program as shown in the figure 8.

Peripheral tissues also contain functional circadian oscillators that are self-sustained at a single cell level but they do not respond to light-dark cycles and appear to require other non-photic physiological stimuli such as food or physical activity in order to sustain their circadian rhythm. In other words clocks within a particular tissue must behave synchronously in order to cohesively regulate organ function. For example, insulin producing β-cells in pancreas influence clock timing in glucagon producing cells so that insulin and glucagon release is timed appropriately in response to food.

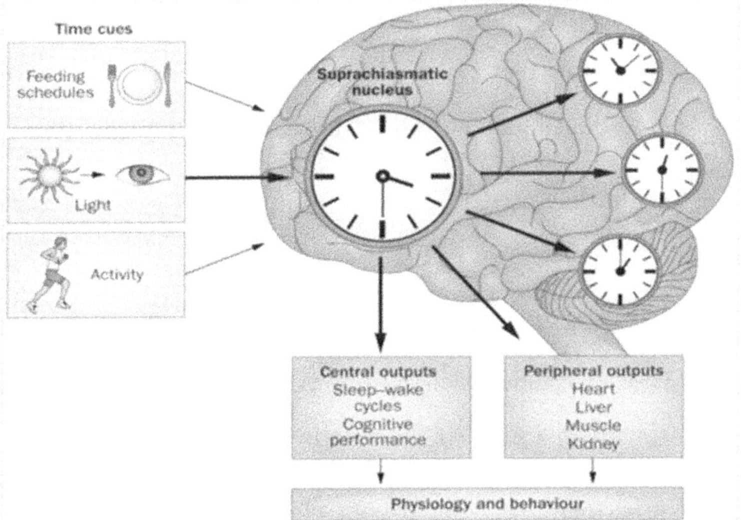

Figure 8: The mammalian clock: The central clock in SCN and peripheral clocks in various tissues together constitute mammalian clock system which is regulated by light, food and activity. (Adapted from: www.pathwayz.org)

Summary

- Circadian oscillators are networks of biochemical feedback loops that generate 24 hour rhythms in organisms ranging from bacteria to plants to vertebrates.

- A given circadian oscillator consists of an auto-regulatory network of multiple transcriptional translational feedback loops where the clock genes are activated or repressed by the rhythmic cycling of the proteins encoded by them.

- The plant circadian clock comprises genes encoding proteins that establish a series of interlocked negative feedback loops which form a regulatory oscillator.

- Multiple oscillators are present in *Neurospora* as well as in *Cyanobacteria*.

- The circadian network in *Drosophila* consists of multiple self-sustained cell autonomous circadian oscillators with a pacemaker function in most of the cells.

- In mammals, the master clock controlling circadian rhythms resides in the suprachiasmatic nucleus (SCN) of the anterior hypothalamus, which plays a crucial role in maintenance of systematic endogenous regulatory factors.

Exercise

A] Multiple Choice Questions:

1. The basic structure of many circadian systems is composed of _________ located within the cell.

    a. Photoreceptor
    b. Clock
    c. Central oscillator

2. In plants, photoreceptors ________ and ________ are involved in setting the clock.

    a. Phytochromes and pacemakers

    b. Cryptochromes and genes

    c. Phytochromes and cryptochromes

3. ________ is the direct photoreceptor organ in *Drosophila*.

    a. Phytochrome

    b. Cryptochrome

    c. Compound eye

4. In mammals, the master clock controlling circadian rhythm resides in the ________.

    a. Ocelli

    b. Suprachiasmatic nucleus

    c. Biochemical oscillator

5. A 'neuroendocrine-loop model' has been proposed to explain

    a. Avian circadian organization

    b. Mammalian circadian organization

    c. Molluscan circadian organization

B] Answer the following:

1. Give an account of basic components of the circadian system.

2. Which are the core circadian oscillators in *Neurospora* and *Cyanobacteria*?

3. Give the working of a circadian clock in *Drosophila*.

4. Write a note on Suprachiasmatic nucleus.

C] Activity:

1. Set the culture of any model organism to study the circadian behaviour.

2. Dissect and observe structural components of the internal clock of given model organism.

Glossary

Endogenous Self - Sustained Oscillator (ESSO):

A mechanism that produces rhythmic (repetitive) variations and can continue to do so for numerous repetitions without external influences

Oscillator:

It is a set of components within a cell, whose action and regulatory interaction are sufficient to produce a rhythm.

Overt rhythm:

A rhythm is an observable characteristic that is directly or indirectly linked to and controlled by the actual pacemaker.

Pacemaker:

a. A localizable, functional anatomical region capable of both sustaining its own oscillations and of entraining other oscillations.

b. The functional unit capable of self-sustaining oscillations, which synchronize other rhythms or internal mechanisms, which sets the period and phase of the endogenous rhythm.

c. They are oscillators which generate biological rhythms in the absence of external periodic inputs.

SCN:

The suprachiasmatic nucleus of the ventral hypothalamus; the chief mammalian circadian pacemaker; the master clock.

References

- T.Kondo and M. Ishiura,"The circadian clock of cyanobacteria," (in eng), Bioessays, vol. 22, no. 1, pp. 10-5, Jan 2000, doi: 10.1002/ (SICI)1521-1878(200001)22:1<10::AID-BIES4>3.0.CO;2-A.

- R. Saini, M. Jaskolski, and S. J. Davis, "Circadian oscillator proteins across the kingdoms of life: structural aspects," (in eng), BMC Biol, vol. 17, no. 1, p. 13, 02 2019, doi: 10.1186/ s12915-018-0623-3.

- T.Schafmeier andA.C.Diernfellner,"Light input and processing in the circadian clock of Neurospora," (in eng), FEBS Lett, vol. 585, no. 10, pp. 1467-73, May 2011, doi: 10.1016/j.febslet.2011.03.050.

6 REGULATION OF ULTRADIAN AND CIRCANNUAL RHYTHMS

Introduction

Biological rhythms other than circadian rhythms are not well understood. Though all rhythms work in synchronization and required for final output, we are not in position to study them together due to experimental complexity. Ultradian rhythms supposed to fine tune the overall output whereas infradian rhythms are necessary to deal with the seasonal changes. Circadian biology is the word synonymously used for Chronobiology due to absence of unambiguous experimental proofs of ultradian and infradian biology. Hormonal secretions or heart beat and bird migration or animal hibernation are the well-known examples of ultradian and circannual rhythms respectively. Now there is a growing attention in research community about temporal understanding of various biological processes, we may expect to get the insight about the molecular players involved in various types of rhythms.

Ultradian rhythms

Ultradian rhythms (URs) have been defined by Daan and Aschoff as short-term rhythms with a frequency of 1×10^{-3} to

5×10^{-5} Hz, that is, with periods in the range of 20 min to 6 h which are shorter than circadian rhythms. Ultradian rhythms were first described by Symansky in 1920 while studying the behavior of fish and rodents. The early data on ultradian rhythms were mostly behavioral observations, as the technology to continuously monitor physiological parameters was not yet developed. Now with sophisticated data collection systems, ultradian rhythms have now been described for body temperature, blood flow, and many other physiological parameters.

Ultradian rhythms in biological processes have been detected in most living organisms and at every level of biological complexity, from eukaryotic microbes such as *Caenorhabditis elegans*, to metazoans including birds and mammals. The great variability in frequency, and the progressive elongation of intervals observed in these rhythms render their interpretation difficult. For many reasons, the term "ultradian rhythms" is inappropriate for the phenomena because URs are aperiodic and termed as Episodic Ultradian Events (EUE). As EUEs tend to occur at erratic frequencies, experimental demonstration is still awaited. Therefore, the mechanisms behind the origin and regulation of EUEs are not as well studied as those of circadian rhythms. Nevertheless, accumulating evidence suggests that the generation of EUEs has a cellular basis.

The EUEs persist despite the removal of potential zeitgebers such as light, food access, and sleep suggests that the EUEs are endogenously generated, rather than behaviorally or environmentally generated. Thus EUEs are independent of zeitgebers and not generated by the same molecular clocks that are responsible for the circadian rhythms. Hence till recently, ultradian events in biological activities have often been dismissed as background noise. While the homeostatic value of seasonal and circadian rhythms is clear because they adapt animals to changes in the environment, the biological significance of ultradian episodes has been questioned, and even neglected as irrelevant.

Functional ultradian oscillators certainly exist at the cellular level. The *Hes* genes in vertebrates encode a family of basic helix-loop-helix transcriptional repressor, the protein product of which inhibits its own mRNA expression and so generates regularly timed oscillations. Like the circadian system, the ultradian Hes1 oscillator is based on a transcriptional–translational feedback mechanism, and the two systems appear similarly regulated. Emerging data argue towards the existence of a global ultradian oscillator that coordinates EUEs across body systems.

Biological relevance of UR/EUE

While there is not yet scientific consensus on the anatomical location of a master ultradian oscillator, accumulating evidence implicates midbrain dopaminergic neurons, orexin neurons, and perhaps the SubParaVentricular-Paraventricular (SPZ-PVN) region are involved in the coordination of physiological EUEs. Biological relevance of EUEs still remains an open question. There is some consensus in the literature on the adaptive value of EUEs, at least for the EUEs of activity and other behaviors. In mammals, the endocrine system is one of the major signaling systems to use frequency encoding through ultradian rhythms.

Like other biological rhythms, the functional significance of EUEs might be in optimizing biological activities by:

(1) Synchronizing compatible processes, and preventing the simultaneous activation of incompatible processes.

(2) Preparing biological systems to respond to stimuli such as cell–cell communication and maintenance of neuronal integrity and alertness.

(3) Interacting with circadian rhythms.

Circannual rhythms

Life on earth has evolved in a periodic world, predictably between conditions that are favorable or unfavorable for an organism. Organisms use favorable seasons to reproduce and grow, and withdraw during unfavorable seasons. To deal with the changes in their environments, all taxonomic groups have evolved genetically programmed timing mechanisms. These govern seasonal cycles in physiology and behaviour that optimize survival and reproductive success, and have been described under umbrella term of circannual rhythms which may be further classified based on the periodicity. Except equatorial regions other parts of the earth undergo annual cycles of exposure to the sun because of the tilt of earth's axis (23.5^0) relative to its orbit around the sun as shown in figure 9. By undergoing pervasive seasonal changes, the biotic environment effectively potentiates geophysical cycles.

Its rhythmicity fundamentally affects the quantity and quality of available food, as well as risks such as predation and infection. These factors have been termed primary causes of sseasonal life histories because they exert selection pressure on individuals and thereby drive evolution.

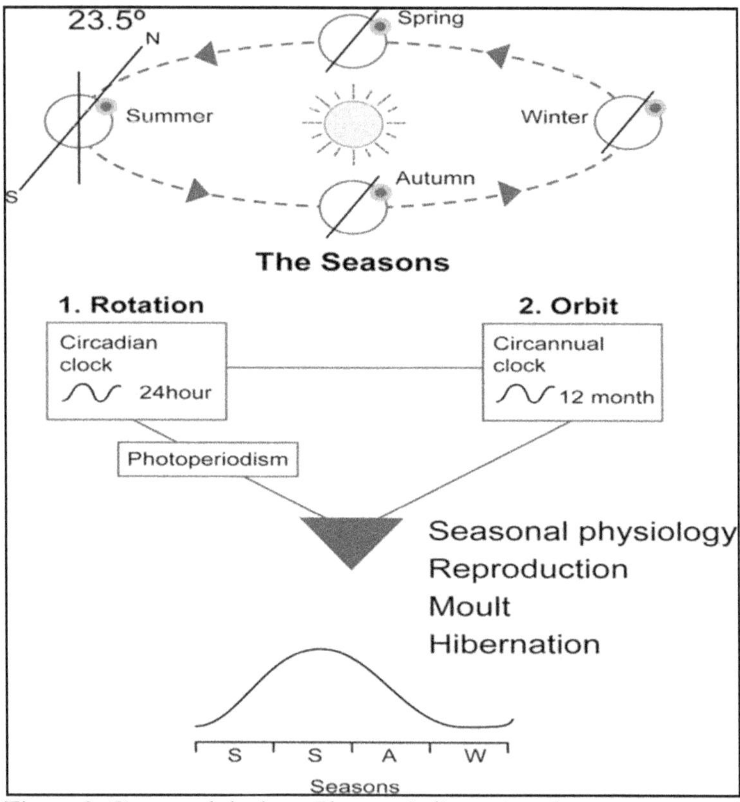

Figure 9: Circannual rhythms: Photoperiodism primarily governs seasonal physiology in plants and animals such as flowering, reproduction, hibernation or migration (Adapted from Biological timekeeping, Ed: Vinod kumar, page no 550)

While circannual rhythms occur within individuals, some can only be characterized at a population level. These include the timing of transitions between modular stages of development in insects. In a typical insect life cycle from egg to larval to pupal to adult, the timing program gates windows of opportunity for developmental transitions that periodically open and close. After the characterization of endogenous circannual rhythms in multicellular organisms, now it is evident that such rhythms are also present in unicellular protists. The marine dinoflagellate, *Alexandrium tamarense*, which is a major contributor to algal bloom (red tide), shows circannual rhythmicity in the propensity of a population of cysts to germinate.

Many circannual studies recorded a set of behavioural and physiological processes within individual subjects, such as, changes in reproductive organs, moult, annual activity patterns and body mass. These processes were shown to recur with period lengths that deviated significantly from the solar year, most typically being short at around 10 months, although in some taxa free-running cycles were consistently longer than 365 days.

Although circannual rhythms free-run under constant conditions, under natural conditions outdoors, they are usually entrained to the Earth's periodicity by annual zeitgebers. Just like circadian rhythms, circannual rhythms have evolved to closely interact with zeitgebers, particularly day length, to adjust the phase and speed of the cycle. Photoperiodism occurs throughout global environments, but responses are generally strong at temperate and high latitudes where the timing of seasonal transitions is predictable, and photoperiod is a reliable zeitgeber. At the equator, where photoperiod is relatively constant throughout the year, non-photic cues such as changes in light intensity between dry and rainy seasons, small changes in the timing of sunrise and sunset, effects of rainfall, food quality and social factors are also strong candidates as zeitgebers.

Circannual biology

The photoperiodic time measurement system consists of three components:

(1) A light input pathway transmitting external light-dark information,

(2) A biological clock measuring photoperiod, and

(3) An output pathway controlling various aspects of physiology and behavior.

Organisms show photoperiodic responses when day length reaches what is called the "critical day length." Most seasonally breeding organisms have highly accurate mechanisms for photoperiodic time measurement and show dramatic seasonal responses to small changes in photoperiod.

Unlike circadian biology, the precise neuroanatomical structures responsible for circannual timing have not been elucidated. Current hypotheses propose that thyrotropes in the pars tuberalis (PT) and/or glial cells in the ependymal layer along the third cerebral ventricle provide circannual timing in vertebrate species. It became apparent that the thyroid gland secreted a key hormone that permitted photoperiodic regulation of circannual rhythms. The localized conversion of thyroxine (T4) into triiodothyronine (T3) in the mediobasal hypothalamus has been shown to be a key event for circannual rhythms in reproductive physiology.

There is an increasing awareness that circannual biology is of economic and medical relevance to humans. Increasing our understanding of annual cycles in farm animals, family pets and wild species is required to help answer many animal welfare and conservation issues. This is of major current interest because of concern about the unknown impact of rapid climate change.

The properties of circannual timing, as compared to circadian timing are enlisted below:

1. Robustness & Innateness: Circannual rhythms, like circadian rhythms, continue in total isolation from environmental rhythmicity thus are endogenous and continue throughout the life cycle.

2. Free-running period: Compared to circadian rhythms, the range of free-running periods and the extent of inter- and intra-individual variation are larger in circannual rhythms.

3. Temperature compensation: Period length of circannual rhythms, like that of circadian rhythms, is largely unaffected by temperature, although more experimental evidence is required.

4. Entrainment: Circannual rhythms, like circadian rhythms, entrain to zeitgebers, are particularly responsive to photic cues.

5. Permissive conditions: The light conditions under which circannual rhythms are expressed are more variable than those of circadian rhythms.

6. Zeitgeber properties: The zeitgeber properties under which circannual rhythms entrain are generally more variable than those of circadian rhythms.

7. Interaction with the circadian system: The circadian system may contribute to circannual rhythm regulation through annually changing external and internal coincidence or simply through measuring day length. An impaired circadian system does not necessarily disrupt circannual rhythmicity (e.g.

SCN-lesioned mammals, pineal-ectomised birds, Arctic damping of clock gene expression).

8. Broad regulatory scope: Circannual rhythms, like circadian rhythms, regulate many processes, including alternation between active and inactive phases.

9. Taxonomic spread: Circannual rhythms, similar to circadian rhythms, are taxonomically widespread.

10. Evolutionary liability: Differences between closely related species suggest that circannual rhythms, like circadian rhythms, are under selection pressure and have high potential for evolutionary change.

Summary

- Like circadian rhythms, ultradian rhythms are also ubiquitous and found in all types of organisms. The great variability in frequency, and the progressive elongation of intervals observed in these rhythms render their interpretation difficult.

- Functional ultradian oscillators exist at the cellular level and recent experimental evidences point towards the existence of a global ultradian oscillator that coordinates EUEs across body systems.

- Circannual rhythms provide optimization in the varying seasons. Along with photoperiod other cues such as humidity, food availability and social factors regulate infradian rhythmicity.

- Unlike circadian biology, the precise neuroanatomical structures responsible for circannual timing have not been elucidated. There are experimental challenges in studying the monthly or yearly rhythms.

- Wild clock studies may be of interest to ecologist and chronobiologists alike.

Exercise:

A] Multiple Choice Questions:

1) Ultradian rhythms are also called -

a) Episodic ultradian events

b) Episodic ultradian rhythms

c) Episodic ultradian activities

d) All of the above

2) Ultradian rhythm ranges from -

a) 1 sec – 23 hrs

b) 1 min – 12 hrs

c) 10 min – 10 hrs

d) 20 min – 6 hrs

3) Fine tuning of various biological rhythms are possible through -

a) Ultradian rhythms

b) Circadian rhythms

c) Circannual rhythms

d) All of the above

4) Primary zeitbeber for circannual rhythm is

a) Meal pattern

b) Humidity

c) Photoperiod

d) Sunrise time

5) Circannual rhythm is under the control of ---------- hormone

a) Melatonin

b) Thyroxine

c) Corticosteriod

d) All of the above

B] Answer the following:

1) Give an account of properties of ultradian rhythm.

2) Compare properties of circadian and circannual rhythms.

3) Explain how organisms get adapted to seasonal variations with examples.

C] Activity:

Observe local varieties of insects/birds/animals for their hibernation/migration/foraging activities.

Glossary

Infradian rhythms:

Having a period length of greater than one day

Photoentrainment:

Entrainment brought about by the action of light cycle.

Photoperiod:

a. The time of light in a light-dark cycle.

b. The length of daylight from dawn to dusk, changing systematically with season depending on geographical location.

Photoperiodic time measurement:

The detection of changes in day length by living organisms.

Photoperiodism:

The use of changes in the day length on an annual basis, and to regulate seasonal behavioral or physiological processes.

Scotoperiod:

The length of darkness from dusk to dawn, changing systematically with season depending on geographical location.

Ultradian rhythms:

Oscillate with a period of less than 20 hours. The frequency of ultradian rhythms varies considerably from one species to another and from one parameter to another.

References

- Episodic Ultradian Events - Ultradian Rhythms Biology 2019, 8, 15; doi:10.3390/biology8010015

- Origin of Ultradian pulsatility in the hypothalamic-pituitary-adrenal axis Proc. R. Soc. B (2010) 277, 1627-1633 doi:10/1098/rspb.2009.2148

- Biological timekeeping, Vinod kumar Ed. (2017)

Cardinal experiment in Chronobiology: Experimental proof for the presence of entrainable endogenous clock.

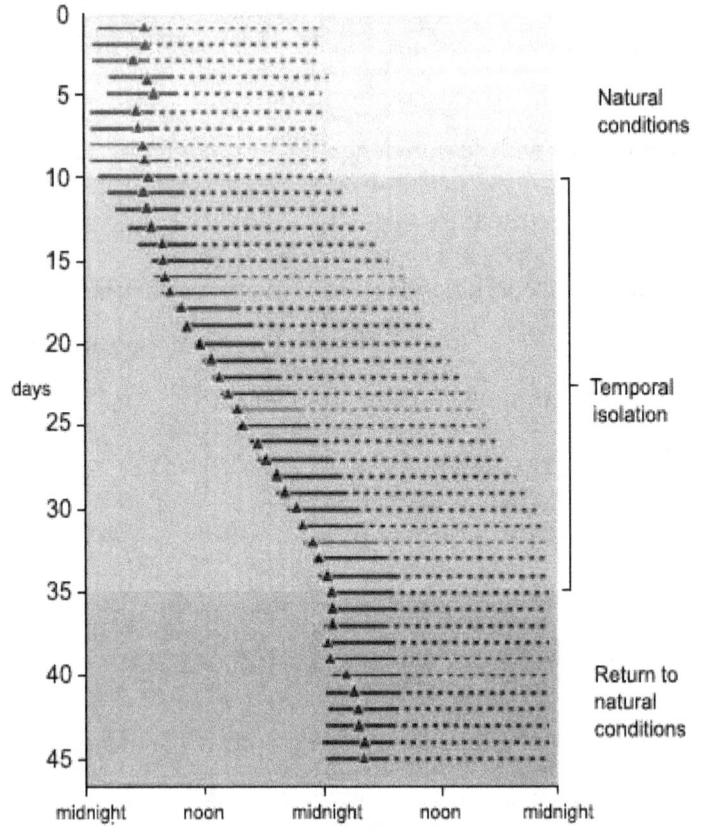

(Dotted line represents rest and Plain line represents activity)

Ref: Chronobiology: Biological Timing edited by Dunlap, Loros & DeCoursey, Published by Sinauer 2004

7 MOLECULAR BASIS OF CIRCADIAN RHYTHM

Introduction

Circadian rhythm appears to be generated at the cellular level which are controlled by endogenous oscillators. It is observed that the rhythms of unicellular organisms are much similar to the rhythms of highly complex mammals. This suggests that a cycle in the activation of certain genes might underlie the timekeeping mechanism. Circadian rhythm is a self-regulating clockwork mechanism that synchronizes oxidative and reductive cycles according to the solar cycle. The main goal of the circadian clock is to coordinate nutrient storage and use it in accordance with the daily period of activity and rest.

Circadian clock

Almost every cell contains an autonomous clock. The core cellular mechanism that generates the circadian oscillator involves transcription-translation feedback loops of clock genes and their protein products.

Entire life is based on proteins, which carry out biochemical functions. The information to encode these proteins is carried on the genes which are the basic unit of inheritance. Core circadian clock genes are defined as genes whose protein products are necessary components for the generation and regulation of circadian rhythms. Clock genes interact with each other in an intricate manner generating oscillations of gene expression.

In other words circadian clock genes are any number of genes that interact with each other to make up an auto regulatory feedback loop, in which its activation and repression cycles take about one day. The underlying principle of circadian clock is successive gene activation in the form of a cycle: the initial activation of a gene is regulated by the last one in the sequence, making up an auto regulatory feedback loop for which one cycle takes about 24 hrs.

Transcription-Translation Feedback Loop (TTFL)

TTFL are hallmarks of circadian clocks in all organisms. In eukaryotes, expression of core clock components is organized in a complex network of interconnected positive and negative feedback loops. This network of gene expression is assumed to generate circadian rhythmicity. TTFL is a negative feedback loop, in which clock genes are regulated by protein products. Generally TTFL involves two main arms: a positive and negative arm.

A positive arm with a heterodimeric complex at its core that behaves as an activator of a system promoting transcription of one or more components of the negative arm which when translated inhibit the activity of the positive arm as shown in figure 10.

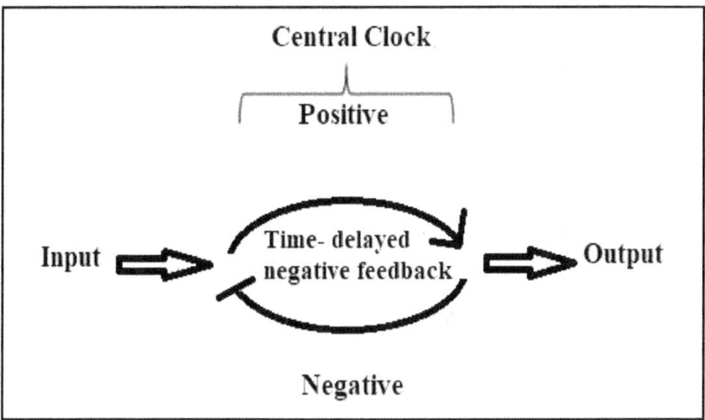

Figure 10: Transcription Translation Feedback Loop: TTFL involves two arms – positive and negative in which clock genes are regulated by protein products which may be regulated by external cues.

When the positive regulatory elements bind to a clock gene promoter, transcription proceed, resulting in a creation of an m-RNA transcript. Then translation proceeds, resulting in a protein product. Once enough protein products accumulate in the cytoplasm, they are transported in a nucleus where they inhibit the positive element from the promoter to stop transcription of clock genes. The clock genes are thus transcribed at low levels until its protein products are degraded. This allows the positive regulatory elements to bind to the promoter and restart transcription.

In short, the positive elements of the loop activate the transcription of clock genes that encode the negative elements and they physically interact with the positive elements to inhibit their activity. This inhibition reduces transcription of genes that encode the negative elements. As a result concentration of negative elements decreases which leads to reactivation of the positive elements allowing the cycle to start again. The negative elements also activate the expression of one or more of the positive elements to form interlocking positive and negative feedback loops that are important for maintaining the stability and robustness of the oscillator.

In the following sections we will learn the transcription-translation feedback loop implicated in clock regulation in *Cyanobacteria, Neurospora crassa, Arabidopsis, Drosophila melanogaster* and rat.

Cyanobacteria

Cyanobacteria are among the oldest organisms on the earth. They were the first prokaryotes reported to have the circadian clock regulated by the cluster of three genes KaiA, KaiB and KaiC. Clock proteins in *Cyanobacteria* generate self-sustained circadian rhythms of auto phosphorylation and dephosphorylation which is independent of transcriptional/ translational feedback. KaiA, KaiB and KaiC proteins are identified as key components of the circadian clock of *Cyanobacteria*.

Conceptual example of the circadian oscillator

In general circadian oscillators are formed from transcription-translation feedback loops. As a conceptual example of this, consider a very simple oscillator with the two components A and B. Genes A and B encode proteins which are the parts of this oscillator. Both these genes regulate each other in a cyclical manner, as one of the genes activates the other and one gene represses the other.

I.   Gene A is expressed in the morning and protein it produces is the activator of gene B.

II. Therefore when a certain amount of protein A has accumulated, gene B is turned on and expressed later in the day.

III. But protein B is a repressor of gene A, so as protein B accumulates, gene A is switched off and protein A levels decrease during the night.

IV. As protein A levels decrease, gene B is turned off.

V.   This releases the repression of gene A by protein B and the expression of gene A begins to increase

Thus the negative feedback regulation of the KaiBC gene expression generating an autonomous oscillation has been considered a key component for the *Cyanobacterial* circadian clock as shown in figure 11.

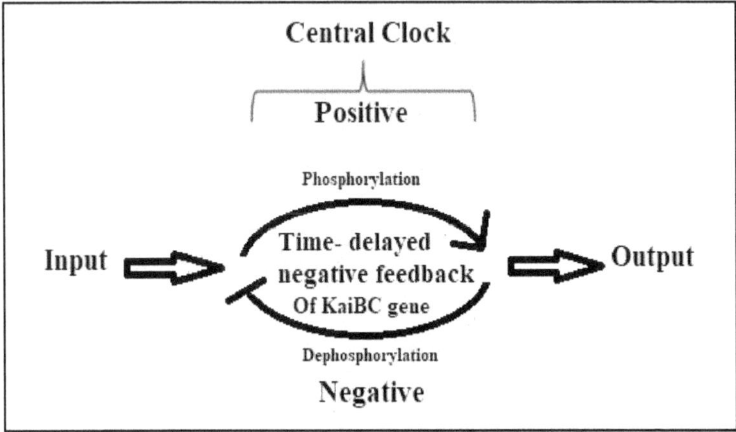

Figure 11 - *Cyanobacteria* circadian clock mechanism

Neurospora crassa

Neurospora is a filamentous fungus classified under the phylum *Ascomycota* and is widely distributed in nature. N. *crassa* formed a model organism in which many of the principles of an oscillator based on transcriptional feedback loops were established as shown in figure 12.

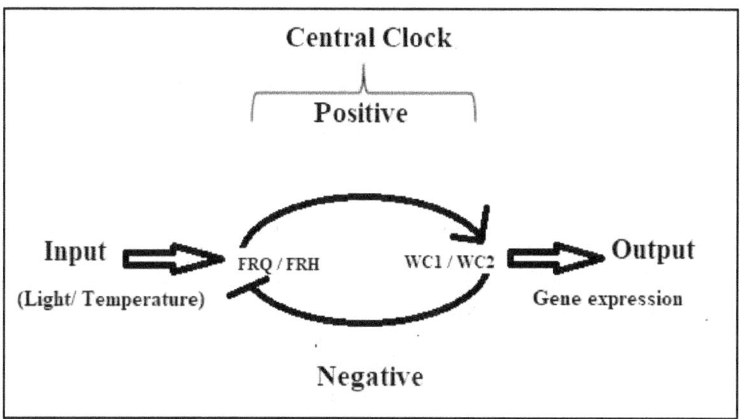

Figure 12 - *Neurospora* circadian clock mechanism

The core circadian oscillator *of Neurospora* consists of an autoregulatory negative feedback loop in which FRQ, FRH, WHITE COLLAR (WC1) and WC2 are the core components. In the negative feedback loop, a complex of FRQ and FRH (FEC) forms a negative arm of the loop, whereas WC1 and WC2 are the positive elements.

Arabidopsis

Plants as poikilothermic, autotrophic and sessile organisms, might be expected to have clocks that are particularly sensitive to environmental variation. The circadian network in the model plant *Arabidopsis thaliana* is notably more complex than those found in animals and fungi. *Arabidopsis thaliana* is a model species for plant physiology and molecular biology research. Consequently, it is the organism in which the molecular mechanism underlying the endogenous clock is best described.

The first molecular model of biological timekeeper in plants was proposed in 2001 for *Arabidopsis thaliana* and was based on a negative transcriptional-translational feedback loop as shown in figure 13. The core loop consists of the Myb-type transcription factors - LATE ELONGATED HYPOCOTYL (LHY) and CIRCADIAN CLOCK ASSOCIATED 1 (CCA1) and the PSEUDO RESPONSE REGULATOR - also known as TIMING OF CAB EXPRESSION1 (TOC1).

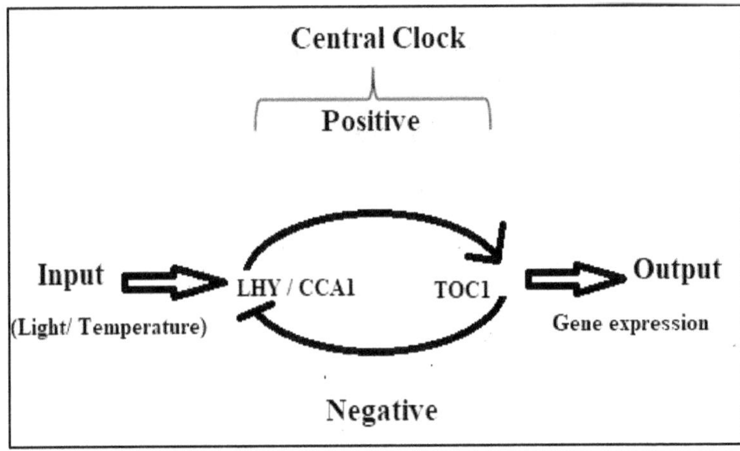

Figure 13 - *Arabidopsis* circadian clock mechanism

Drosophila melanogaster

Drosophila melanogaster has been a model organism of choice to understand genetically, molecularly and at the level of neural circuits how circadian rhythms are generated, how they are synchronized by environmental cues and how they drive behavioral cycles such as locomotor rhythms.

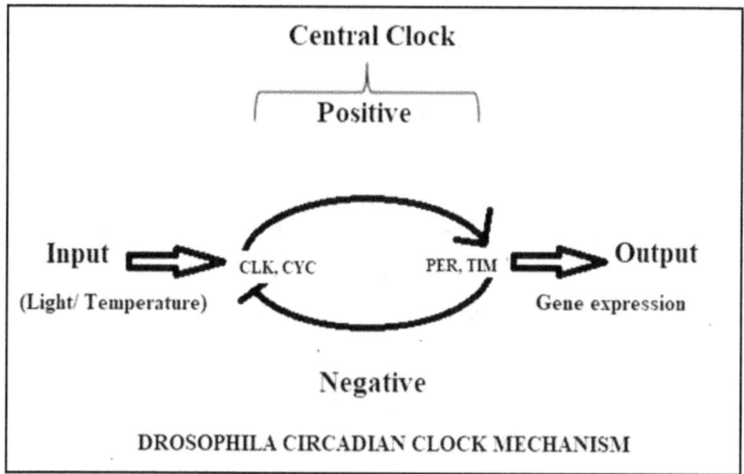

Figure 14 - *Drosophila* circadian clock mechanism

The fruit fly circadian oscillator is composed of two interlocked feedback loops. The circadian genes period (per), timeless (tim), clock (clk) and cycle (cyc) together make up the core transcriptional feedback loop that drives circadian rhythm in *Drosophila* as shown in figure 14.

Rat

As described earlier, in mammals, "The Master Clock " controlling circadian rhythms reside in the suprachiasmatic nucleus (SCN) of the anterior hypothalamus, which plays a crucial role in maintenance of systemic endogenous regulatory factors. A set of 14 genes forms the core-network of the mammalian circadian clock that accounts for the generation of circadian rhythm within the individual cells. These elements are necessary for the robust generation of oscillations, which can occur in the absence of external inputs. All elements in this network interact via positive and negative transcriptional and translational feedback loop. The core TTFL is composed of:

a) Transcriptional activator proteins - Circadian Locomotor Output Cycles Kaput (CLOCK) and Brain and Muscular ARNT-Like1 (BMAL1)

b) Repressor proteins Period1 (PER1), PER2, PER3, Cryptochrome-1(CRY1) and CRY2.

Other loops are coupled to the core TTFL to maintain oscillations. During the early time of circadian day, the heterodimer complex CLOCK/BMAL1 is formed. This leads to the activation of genes PER1, PER2, CRY1 and CRY2. At a later stage, PER and CRY gene products accumulate and form complexes which translocate into the nucleus to interact with CLOCK and BMAL1, repressing their own transcription.

Other loops are coupled to the core TTFL to complete the oscillations. The autoregulatory feedback loop described takes ~24h to complete the cycle and constitute a circadian molecular clock as shown in figure 15.

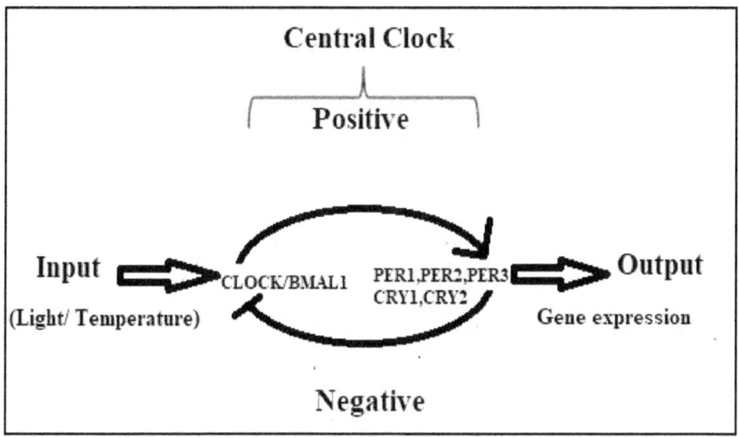

Figure 15 - Rat circadian clock mechanism

Summary

- Circadian rhythms are controlled by an endogenous oscillator, the circadian clock.

- Circadian rhythmicity arises as a cell-autonomous trait even in multicellular organisms.

- Circadian clock constitutes an autoregulatory succession of expression, accumulation and degradation of clock gene products that forms an autonomous molecular oscillator.

- In all clocks, an important negative feedback loop occurs at the transcriptional level. Transcription factors induce the expression of other clock genes that then act to negatively regulate their own transcription, creating oscillating patterns of gene expression.

- In *Cyanobacteria*, the three central oscillator proteins - KaiA, KaiB and KaiC - drive the 24h cyclic gene expression rhythm.

- In *Neurospora crassa* circadian FRQ/WCC oscillator is based on an autoregulatory transcriptional-translational feedback loop.

- A simple version of *Arabidopsis* circadian clock comprises three interlocked feedback loops with two single Myb domain transcription factors CCA1 and LHY, playing roles in each loop.

- In *Drosophila*, the circadian oscillator is composed of two interlocked feedback loops - the original PER/TIM loop and a clock (CLK) loop.

- On the transcriptional level, the degree of feedback repression of the transcription of PER and TIM is a key regulator of the circadian clock in Drosophila.

- In the mammalian circadian clock, the central oscillator is formed by two clusters of neurons and is located in the hypothalamus above the optic chiasma, thus named suprachiasmatic nucleus.

- The core TTFL in mammalian circadian clock is composed of (a) transcriptional activator proteins CLOCK and BMAL1 (b) repressor proteins PER1, PER2, PER3 (c) Cytochrome1 and Cytochrome2.

Exercise

A] Multiple Choice Questions:

1. The circadian rhythms are controlled by _________

   a. TTFL
   b. Oxidative cycle
   c. Circadian oscillator

2. TTFL is a _______ feedback loop.

   a. Positive

   b. Negative

   c. Neutral

3. Circadian rhythm in *Cyanobacteria* _________ of TTFL.

   a. Dependent

   b. Independent

   c. Partially dependent

4. In _Neurospora_, in the negative feedback loop, a complex of FRQ and FRH forms a _______ arm of the loop.

    a. Left

    b. Negative

    c. Positive

5. The core TTFL is composed of _______ and _______ in Rat.

    a. Kai A and Kai B

    b. WC1 and WC2

    c. CLOCK and BMAL1

B] Answer the following:

1. Explain the transcription-translation loop

2. Draw a diagram explaining the molecular mechanism of circadian rhythm of _Neurospora crassa._

3. Give the core components of circadian oscillators in -

    a. _Cyanobacteria_

    b. _Arabidopsis_

    c. _Drosophila_

4. Explain the molecular mechanism of circadian rhythm in rat.

C] Activity:

Generate animation video for molecular mechanism of circadian oscillation of any model organism.

Glossary

Clock controlled genes (CCG) / Clock genes:

A gene whose expression is rhythmically regulated by a clock.

Clock associated genes:

Genes those are not rhythmic but get affected by clock genes.

Transcription Translation Feedback Loop:

TTFL involves two arms – positive and negative in which clock genes are regulated by protein products which may be regulated by external cues.

Circadian oscillator:

Protein products of clock genes involved in TTFL.

References

- J. G. Smith and P. Sassone-Corsi, "Clock-in, clock-out: circadian timekeeping between tissues," (in eng), Biochem

(Lond), vol. 42, no. 2, pp. 6-10, Apr 2020, doi: 10.1042/bio04202007.

- Y. Xie et al., "New Insights Into the Circadian Rhythm and Its Related Diseases," (in eng), Front Physiol, vol. 10, p. 682, 2019, doi: 10.3389/fphys.2019.00682.

- W. Yu and P. E. Hardin, "Circadian oscillators of Drosophila and mammals," (in eng), J Cell Sci, vol. 119, no. Pt 23, pp. 4793-5, Dec 2006, doi: 10.1242/jcs.03174.

- P. F. Devlin, "Signs of the time: environmental input to the circadian clock," (in eng), J Exp Bot, vol. 53, no. 374, pp. 1535-50, Jul 2002, doi: 10.1093/jxb/erf024.

- Y. Serin and N. Acar Tek, "Effect of Circadian Rhythm on Metabolic Processes and the Regulation of Energy Balance," (in eng), Ann Nutr Metab, vol. 74, no. 4, pp. 322-330, 2019, doi: 10.1159/000500071.

- C. H. Ko and J. S. Takahashi, "Molecular components of the mammalian circadian clock," (in eng), Hum Mol Genet, vol. 15 Spec No 2, pp. R271-7, Oct 2006, doi: 10.1093/hmg/ddl207.

PART III

RELEVANCE OF CIRCADIAN SYSTEM IN HUMAN WELFARE

8 LIFESTYLE AND BIOLOGICAL CLOCK

Introduction

Lifestyle is a set of goals, plans, values, attitudes, behaviors and beliefs manifested in the personal and family life of the individual and his social and cultural interactions. It is an interdisciplinary concept which involves a health oriented view of the physical, psychological, social and spiritual aspect of life. Lifestyle consists of day to day common activities of an individual such as sleep and waking time.

As our lifestyles become increasingly demanding, we build our lives around artificially divided days and nights that accommodate the need to work night shifts, stay up all night or travel between continents. But this impacts our natural body clocks, with unwanted consequences. Public health studies are consistently revealing more and more connections between modern lifestyles and our internal biological clock and when those two clash, it can lead to development of diseases.

Lifestyle factors affecting biological clock

There are many external stimuli in modern lifestyle that take us out of synchronization with our circadian rhythm. We cannot avoid them but awareness will help us to choose healthier alternatives as much as possible.

Artificial light

Sunlight is the most powerful entraining signal for the body clock. For thousands of years, our daily habits and routines were determined by the sun. We are diurnal animals and hence our body mechanism is designed to work only during day time. As the sun goes down, the light intensity is reduced. The dimming of light initiates melatonin secretion in the brain, this was the cue for early man to eat and start preparing for sleep.

This pattern is disturbed by modern lifestyle; the blue light that comes off screen mimics the full day light, messing up the secretion of melatonin and ultimately affecting one's sleep pattern. It causes a significant shift in the circadian rhythms which leads to irritability, anxiety, depressive behaviors, also decreasing learning and memory efficiency. We spend most of the time indoors either in office or at home where the light intensity is much less as compared to natural sunlight which confuses the circadian mechanism.

Large eating window

In early human history, food wasn't continuously available. Our bodies are primed to digest and utilize food for roughly 8-10 hours' time period. Eating outside these hours will mean that digestion can take longer and we will process fats and sugar inefficiently. Now-a-days, globally, one's daily light exposure and eating behavior varies with the way of living. The 'long lighted days' have empowered longer eating hours daily.

Large number of genes are expressed diurnally and differentially to regulate daily physiology. Cyclic yet tissue specific expression of genes regulates functional processes. These intracellular processes orchestrate circadian secretion of metabolites. The metabolites and other signaling molecules transcribe information at cellular, tissue and organismal level. The role of circadian pacemaker is to fine tune these processes for all body components. These temporal signals from SCN drive feeding-fasting rhythm, which in turn synchronizes clock genes in peripheral clocks such as liver cells. Importantly, food intake entrains peripheral clocks, including liver, not the SCN; such that intake outside the designated 'temporal' window, leads to asynchrony between peripheral clock and SCN. In this way, nutrient metabolism is under circadian regulation. Regardless of what we eat, what time we eat matters. Our body is not only influenced by light and dark, but also by the timing of our meals.

There are two sets of processes that need to go on in a cell. Cells need to take up nutrients and process them for energy to fuel the work that the cell needs to do. And the other half of the, which is night for us, is for growth and repair. Eating sends a cue to the body's cells that is 'day' and time to take up nutrients. But if we eat late at night or in the wee hours of the morning then the clock in the body's cells may get confused and miss out on the night process.

If the body cannot undergo proper growth and repair, if the damage to the cells that has accumulated in the metabolic processes are not being fixed up, then the possibilities to get abnormalities are more. Food plays a major role and not only calorie intake but the timing of intake is also important. Circadian schedule can be summarized as follows.

It is best to have a balanced and sumptuous breakfast in the morning, as it prevents binging during the day. It is also good to drink water and fresh juice through the mid-morning and have an early lunch when the sun is at its peak. As the sun starts setting, one should reduce the portion of food and have an early dinner.

Today many of us have our biggest meal at dinner, just when the body needs the least energy and when bowel movements are suppressed. This way, most of the food gets stored as fat. Thus eating at the wrong times could have a major impact on our circadian rhythms. By time-restricted feeding, we are resetting the circadian clock back to where it should be and which is important for the overall health.

Inconsistent bed/waking time

Human circadian rhythm is governed by routine. We need to be waking up at the same time every single morning, including weekends, consistently optimizing the quality and efficiency of our sleep. Unfortunately, the modern lifestyle does not promote consistent sleeping habits. Our social commitments and availability of 24x7 entertainment industry take us out of sync with the natural light/dark cycle of the sun. Important crucial processes of health and well-being are largely tied to the natural light that comes from the Sun's rays that is picked up by the central biological clock in the brain. When sunlight comes in through the eyes, the SCN picks up the cue that its daylight and time to get up and be active.

As the light diminishes and then disappears, the clock signals the body that it is time to sleep. As there is a direct relationship between uncertain sleep-waking times and disrupted circadian rhythm, the unregulated schedules can increase the risk of chronic diseases.

Lifestyle changes for tuning of biological clock

Biological clock is governed by light, diet and exercise. The circadian time system is robust enough to fine tune itself and is in most of the cases it can regain the balance without any medication. While the circadian rhythm is susceptible to disturbances, it can still be brought back with simple lifestyle changes as described below.

1) Enhance natural light exposure

Reduced exposure to sunlight impairs circadian rhythms. It is important that one should be exposed to natural light especially in the morning and as much as possible throughout the day. In addition to helping the circadian system, this will also help to get a healthy dose of Vitamin D, which has its own circadian rhythm syncing properties.

2) Get Outdoors

It is important to expose yourself to natural light throughout the day once in a while. Research shows that taking couple of days to go camping where one has no access to electronics or even watches (allowing the sun to dictate when to rise and when to go to sleep) can greatly affect the sleep-wake cycle.

3) Physical activity

During the day, our muscles are primed for activity. Moving as much as possible throughout the daylight hours is an effective way to keep the circadian rhythm in check. Make a habit of moving around after each meal for a while. Avoid long stretches of sedentary work at desk. This habit will help synchronization of muscle clock.

4) Practice good sleep hygiene

This is probably one of the most powerful ways to take control of the circadian rhythm. Go to bed and wake up at the same time every single day. Sleep is the most important drug for tuning of circadian rhythm.

5) Eat at set times

Researchers believe that eating within a restricted time period provides the digestive system the right amount of time to perform its function uninterrupted by a new influx of food. It also gets enough time to repair and rejuvenate, supporting the growth of healthy bacteria in the gut.

6) Optimizing gut health

Emerging research indicates that intestinal cells and gut microbes have their own circadian rhythms that interact with bodily rhythms; this means that we can improve our gut health by taking care of our circadian system and vice versa. Eating an anti-inflammatory nutrient dense diet can normalize gut microbe rhythms and improve gut health.

7) Manage stress

Higher stress levels offset stress hormone and melatonin levels, leading to more dysfunction of the internal clock. Learn to avoid unmanageable and manage unavoidable. Mindfulness techniques of your choice would help to limit stress before it reaches alarming level.

Need for changing lifestyle

There is a pattern and unique rhythm in nature, which depends on the sun. Our body has been following this rhythm forever and breaking it causes disturbances. In the modern world it is difficult to keep in touch with the regular natural cycles and the circadian cycles are generally ignored or altered. For example, women taking birth control pills which also has altered their menstrual cycle. The natural circadian cycle has also been altered due to our changing habitat; we live in an era where air conditionings provides cooling during summers and we have heaters to provide warmth during winters. It can be said that we have started commanding our nature and stopped being the slave of our circadian cycles. Increasing digestive problems and problems of headache and other mild diseases show the impact of the imbalance created by modern lifestyle.

Current lifestyle is not sustainable because we are exploiting the resources by technological advances which disturbs the internal as well external environment. Circadian lifestyle will improve our efficiency and tunes the internal time mechanism.

Summary

- Modern life challenges to our circadian system present a long term threat to our health.

- Humans are not evolved for night shifts, nighttime lights and intercontinental travel.

- Lifestyle is a major determinant of circadian health and relates to people's psychosomatic factors, feeding-fasting, activity-rest, sleep-wake routines.

- Today's modern technology makes social and work activities independent of the environment's light/dark duration. Hence long flight across continents (jet lag), shift work and night work as kinds of habits of modern lives can influence circadian rhythm function.

- Any aberration in light-dark cycle or feeding-fasting cycle accrues adverse effects on the body clocks leading to circadian disruption.

- Manufacturing, Service or IT industry has multifold shifts creating 'light at night' cities. It is viewed as a cause of circadian disruption; there are other unseen factors as well.

- Besides, daily work routine and fast food popularity have contributed to circadian disruption, variation in daily rhythms of eating and sleep, enhancing disease consequences.

Exercise

A] Multiple Choice Questions:

1. ______ is the most powerful entertaining signal for the body clock.

    a. Moonlight
    b. Sunlight
    c. Artificial light

2. Our body is not only influenced by light and dark, but also by the ______ of our meals.

    a. Quality
    b. Quantity
    c. Timing

3. As the sun starts setting, one should ______ the portion of food.

    a. Increase
    b. Reduce
    c. Make no change in

4. When we work late at night, with the help of electrical lights, our body photoreceptors sense light and slowly suppress ______ .

    a. Creatinine
    b. Cortisol
    c. Melatonin

5. For good sleep hygiene, one should avoid _______ in the evening.

   a. Coffee / Tea
   b. Milk
   c. Fruit juice

B] Answer the following:

1. Describe the role of artificial light that takes us out of sync with our circadian rhythm.

2. With any four points explain how circadian rhythm can be brought back with simple lifestyle changes.

3. Circadian rhythm is influenced by the timings of our meals. Explain.

4. Why is there a need to change our lifestyle?

C] Activity:

Observing your own biological rhythms:

You can select any parameter and make your own observations and report.

1) Observing your nasal cycle – (Breathing pattern by left/right nostril) Note down the active nostril when you wake up, during

lunch time and while going to bed at night. Make 3 observations per day for at least 7 days.

2) Observing your body temperature – Observe, measure your body temperature and plot the graph of body temperature vs time. Note down when you the temperature when you wake up, after lunch, evening between 5-7 pm and while going to bed at night. Make 4 observations per day for at least 7 days.

3) Observing your body pulse rate – Observe, measure your pulse rate and plot the graph of pulse rate vs time. Note down pulse rate when you wake up, after lunch, evening between 5-7 pm and while going to bed in the night. Make 4 observations per day for at least 7 days.

References

- D. Farhud and Z. Aryan, "Circadian Rhythm, Lifestyle and Health: A Narrative Review," (in eng), Iran J Public Health, vol. 47, no. 8, pp. 1068-1076, Aug 2018.

- N. J. Gupta, "Lifestyle and Circadian Health: Where the Challenges Lie?," (in eng), Nutr Metab Insights, vol. 12, p. 1178638819869024, 2019, doi: 10.1177/1178638819869024.

9 CIRCADIAN RHYTHM DISORDERS

Introduction

Circadian clock is a major regulating factor for nearly all physiological activities and its disorder has severe consequences on human health. Circadian timing system or circadian clock mechanism plays a crucial role in many biological processes such as sleep-wake cycle, cardiovascular health, glucose homeostasis, hormonal secretion and body temperature. When circadian systems are disrupted by genetic or other environmental defects, dysfunction of various physiological processes can occur. Thus circadian rhythms play an integral role in diverse aspects of physical and mental health.

Reasons for disruption of circadian rhythm

Circadian rhythm can undergo free run in the absence of the source of entrainment. However misalignment of internal oscillations with the external environment results in the circadian desynchronization. It is caused by circadian misalignment between internal clock and external cues or loss of rhythmicity due to deregulation of clock genes. In other words circadian rhythm disruption is caused by erratic behavior or by conflicting timing of our internal rhythms and our environment.

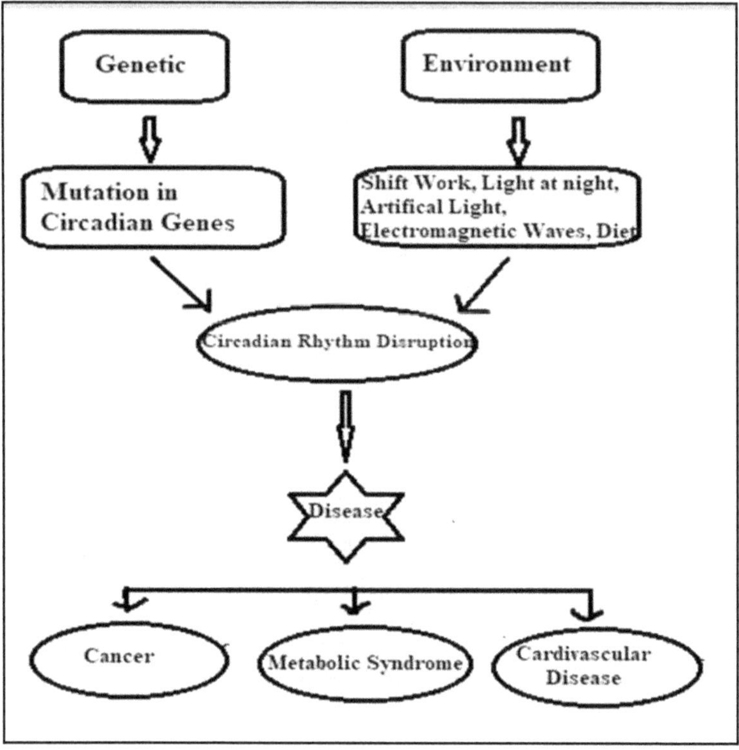

Figure16: Circadian rhythm disorders. There are environmental as well as genetic factors associated with various types of circadian rhythm disorders which are still not explicitly correlated with lifestyle disorders.

Circadian rhythm is controlled by a cyclic expression of circadian genes and mutation in these genes results in the disruption of the circadian oscillator. Thus, circadian rhythm disruption occurs by both genetic as well as environmental factors as described in figure 16.

Circadian rhythm disorders

Due to disruption in circadian rhythm one may experience both short term and long term consequences of health conditions.

Long term consequences includes disruption in circadian rhythm can cause health conditions in several parts of the body in the long run. This includes various organs, cardiovascular system metabolism, gastrointestinal system, skin etc. One may become susceptible to diabetes, obesity, and mental health conditions as well. Short term consequences includes Short term disruption in circadian rhythms may result in problems with memory and lack of energy.

Some of the genes involved in regulating circadian rhythms are also part of other cell pathways. Disruption/ malfunctioning of such genes can affects circadian rhythms as well as other cellular processes. One of the processes regulated by the circadian clock is the cell cycle. Therefore cancerous cells which undergo abnormal cell division are due to disruption of circadian rhythm.

Circadian rhythm disruption may be a potential contributor in obstructive sleep apnea (OSA) a sleep disorder marked by repeated lapse in breathing. OSA reduces body oxygen level and causes numerous sleep interruptions throughout the night.

Changes in our body and environmental factors can cause our circadian rhythm and the natural light dark cycle to be out of synchronization. These changes can cause sleep disorders and may lead to other chronic health conditions such as obesity, diabetes, depression, bipolar disorder, and several affective disorders. The most important disorder of circadian rhythm is sleep disturbance. In humans, dysfunction or misalignments of the circadian clock with environmental cues alter the timings of the sleep-wake cycle leading to a variety of circadian rhythm sleep disorders.

Types of circadian rhythm disorders

Circadian rhythm cycles become active everyday with regularity between sleepiness and alertness that is known as sleep-wake cycle. Modern lifestyle does not allow to follow consistent sleep-wake cycle which is the primary reason of circadian rhythm disorders.

Delayed Sleep Phase Disorder (DSPD)

This type of circadian disorder is associated with night owls who stay up late at night and sleep late in the morning. In this condition the endogenous circadian pacemaker is not aligned to the desired sleep-wake cycle with sleep and wake occurring earlier or later than desired.

This desynchrony is referred to as phase misalignment and is thought to arise due to delay in the circadian pacemaker. DSPD causes longer than normal circadian period (eg. 25 hr.). The exact cause of DSPD is unknown but may be related to genetics, underlying physical conditions and a person's behavior. It is associated with a number of negative health consequences and significant functional impairments like job performance, financial difficulties, and marital problems in adults.

Advanced Sleep Phase Disorder (ASPD)

This is a rare disorder as compared to DSPD which is characterized by 3-4 hour advanced sleep onset and wake times relative to desired normal times on most nights. People with this type of disruption find that they get tired early in the evening and wake up very early in the morning. Even if they want to be up late at night or sleep later in the morning, people with advanced sleep phase disorder usually cannot do so.

It may be associated with a shorter than normal circadian period (< 24 hr). Its prevalence in the general population increases with age. In some cases, advanced sleep phase disorder may be related to an inherited genetic cause and inefficiency of functioning of master clock in brain.

Irregular Sleep-Wake Rhythm Disorder

Persons affected by the Irregular sleep-wake rhythm disorder have an undefined pattern of sleep-wake rhythm. People with this rare disorder have no consistent pattern of their sleep and may have many naps or short sleeping periods throughout the day instead of one consolidated sleep period.

It is frequently connected to conditions that affect the brain such as dementia or traumatic brain injury, that limit the proper functioning of the master clock in the hypothalamus. It is the result of inadequate sleep hygiene and lack of exposure to synchronizing external agents such as sunlight, physical and social activities.

Non-24 h Sleep-Wake Disorder / Free Running type Circadian Rhythm Sleep Disorder

This disorder is also known as non-entrained or free running type circadian rhythm sleep disorder. This is characterized by sleep symptoms that occur as a result of the longer (approximately 25 h) duration of the circadian timing mechanism cycle. Lack of light signal in individuals unable to receive the light-dark external cues for the circadian clock system is one major factor causing this syndrome in which individuals do not keep a regular 24 hr sleep-wake schedule.

This condition occurs primarily in blind people and therefore is not able to receive light-based cues for their circadian rhythm. Their body still follows a 24-h cycle, but their sleeping hours constantly shift backwards by minutes or hours at a time. The disorder can become chronic if left untreated. It can also lead to depressive symptoms and mood disorders. Such syndrome is common in blind persons and individuals with irregular light-dark patterns because of night shifts or rotating schedules.

Circadian Rhythm Sleep disorder Due to Work at Irregular Hours

Jet lag and Shift work associated disorders are considered as circadian rhythm sleep disorders in the latest classification of sleep disorders (ICSD-3) released in 2014.

Jet lag disorders – Jet lag is a temporary phase resulting from normal response of the body to changing time zones faster than the body can adjust. This happens when a person crosses a lot of time zones in a short period of time, during intercontinental flights. When a person crosses different time zones, the internal body clock will be different from the local time. The body clock will eventually reset itself, but this often takes a few days after the arrival and resolves spontaneously within one week to align with a new time zone.

Jet lag is caused by the temporary divergence between the environmentally adequate sleep-wake cycle and the endogenous cycle generated by the circadian timing mechanisms. When jet lag sets in, the person feels disoriented, foggy and sleepy at the wrong times of the day. The affected people complain of insomnia or sleepiness, impaired alertness, cognitive problems, fatigue, mental dysfunction, tiredness, loss of concentration, anxiety, depression, irritability, mood disorder and gastrointestinal illness.

This disorder affects all age groups, though older people can present more pronounced symptoms. The severity of the jet lag symptoms correlates with the number of time zones crossed. More the number of time zones, the more severe the symptoms are. It has been known that jet lag causes a shift in behavioural, physiological and hormonal rhythms in humans.

<u>Treatment of jet lag</u> – Most people do not require treatment for jet lag and their bodies naturally adapt after a short period in the new time zone. It is possible to increase the rate of adaptation of the body clock to a new time zone using specifically time exposure to bright light and/or specifically time treatment with the hormone called melatonin.

Timed exposure to bright light, before flying out and for the first 3-4 days after flight should start and speed up the internal time clock's adjustment to the new location. Timed treatment with melatonin pre and post flight in the early morning of the departure time zone (westward) or the very early evening of the departure time zone (eastward) may also help body clock adjustment. At the same time, it is important to change behavior such as eating and sleeping to coincide with the new time zone. Once the internal clock has adapted, the jet lag problem resolves.

<u>Other types of Jet lag</u> – It is not only the change in time zone but our life style choices also misaligns our daily rhythms and gives us the experience of jet lag which affect body in similar way like traditional jet lag.

Digital jet lag – when our body is in a one-time zone but the mind is in another zone.

Metabolic jet lag – If we change food intake timing frequently, the body may experience what we may call metabolic jet lag.

Social Jet lag – The most unrecognized and most prevalent type of circadian disruption is social jetlag, which could affect more than 50% of us. Due to social compulsions we tend to change the sleep and meal timings on free days which lead to social jet lag.

Shift work disorders

Shift work disorder is another example of how we can get ourselves off-cycle, and this too can develop into circadian rhythm disorder, over the long term. The invention of electric lights has made light omnipresent 24 hrs a day and permitted round the clock shift work. Shift work sleep disorder commonly affects those who work non-traditional hours, outside the typical 9am to 5pm work day.

Many people across the world are employed as shift workers and are forced to adapt a work rest schedule that does not match the 24 hour solar day resulting in 'circadian misalignment. Engaging in shift work often induces conflict between people's internal body clock and actual time of the day. Conflicts make the shift worker work when their body is preparing for sleep and sleep when their body is preparing for wakefulness.

Working at irregular hours often causes sleep disorders characterized by complaints of insomnia, excessive sleepiness, shortened total sleep time and inadequate sleep quality. Besides impairing work performance, this disorder also increases the risk of accidents due to decreased alertness. People who work the night shift not only have a hard time with their sleep patterns but other systems in their body also feel the effects.

This disorder also causes physical and mental health diseases such as hypertension, breast cancer, uterine and cervical cancer and cardiovascular disorders.

Night shift work is a real health hazard as shift workers favor irregular eating times and is therefore associated with altered insulin sensitivity, and higher body mass leading to increased risk of obesity and inflammation. Further, night shift work is clearly most important in certain occupations like healthcare and aviation industries where people are mostly awake for many hours and are often unable to maintain sleep patterns that correspond to the natural human circadian rhythm. This may develop fatigue leading to many accidents and unwanted situations. Many studies have shown that the development of metabolic syndrome and incidences of coronary heart diseases are strongly associated with nurses working in the night shifts.

<u>Ways to lessen the effects of shift work sleep disorders</u> – The individual tolerance to effects of shift work remains a complex problem. Some studies have shown that shift work can adversely affect an individual's bodily rhythms, while there are studies showing varied tolerance of the effects of shift work from person to person. Not everyone who works in a non-traditional shift, experiences shift work sleep disorder. Many people who work these shifts have circadian rhythms that make them natural 'night owls' and hence are able to avoid the disorder. Age, gender also play a role and varied tolerance is seen. Shift work is going affect our body in long run. If we

cannot change the job, we only hope to reduce its side effects to certain extent by following practices:

- Try to keep a regular sleep schedule, including on days off
- If possible, take 48 hours off after a series of shifts
- Use sunglasses to minimize sun exposure
- Take a nap whenever possible
- Limit caffeine intake for hours before bed time
- Maintain a healthy diet rich in fruits and vegetables
- Use heavy shades for sleeping to create a dark environment
- Sleeping in a noiseless or minimal noise environment
- Avoid long commutes to avoid further drowsiness
- Keep nightly rituals before bed, even during the daytime
- Take over-the-counter melatonin as per doctor's prescription
- Use of light box therapy for exposure to safe light before work shift
- Take a 30 to 60 minutes nap right before your shift

Circadian rhythm and women's health

Women are susceptible to and affected by circadian rhythm disruption is reported at nearly twice the rate than men. The regulation of circadian rhythm particularly in the sleep-wake cycle, is an important aspect of women's health to consider especially as it relates to fertility and menopause. Shift workers have an increased rate of infertility (11.3%) in addition to an increased rate of menstrual disruption (16.09%). Circadian rhythm disruption has the ability to impact conception.

Women going through menopause often experience insomnia; this is partially due to reduced levels of hormones like estrogen and progesterone, both of which have sleep protective benefits. However, insomnia associated with the menopause may be additionally influenced by reduced levels of melatonin that have been shown to decrease with age, specifically as women approach menopause. As the circadian rhythm greatly influences the production of melatonin, the disturbance of the circadian system is of substantial relevance to the direct impairment of sleep regulation in menopausal and post-menopausal women.

Recommendations to maintain healthy circadian rhythm

Most of the lifestyle disorders we face today has found to have associated circadian dysfunction. We should be more aware about bodily rhythmic behavior and make a practice to note down the change in any rhythmic pattern in daily routine. The circadian lifestyle summarized below will help us to tune our internal time mechanism.

1. Adequate exposure to sunlight
2. Consistent daily routine and sleep/wake cycle
3. Regular Outdoor activity

4. Limiting artificial light exposure after sunset

5. Limiting day time nap maximum to 20 min

6. Consistent meal timings with restricted eating window

7. Effective management of stressful situations

Summary

- A circadian rhythm is an endogenously driven oscillating biological rhythm that resets approximately every 24 hours and can synchronize the body functions with the external temporal environment by photic (light) and non-photic (for example, temperature, food, exercise) cues.

- Several environmental and genetic factors can cause disruption of the circadian rhythms. This disruption could contribute to multifactorial diseases such as cancer, cardiovascular disease and metabolic syndrome.

- Disruption to the circadian clock may contribute to health problems. This occurs for example, during night shift work or jet lag, in which there is a mismatch between light exposures, food intake and other cues from the external environment with the timing of the circadian rhythms in the body.

- Circadian rhythm helps control daily schedules for sleep and wakefulness.

- We can maintain a healthy clock by eating within 10-12 hours/day, getting exposure to sunlight in the morning, trying to go to bed and wake up at the same time each day and exercising regularly.

- Jet lag disorder is a recognized circadian rhythm sleep disorder characterized by insomnia or excessive daytime sleepiness associated with transmeridian jet travel and also by inconsistent daily schedule.

- When considering the impact of shift work on health and wellbeing, it is also essential to consider the effects of behavioral, societal and environmental forces that may ameliorate or exacerbate the biological consequences of circadian misalignment.

Exercise:

A] Multiple choice questions:

1. ________ disorder is associated with a shorter than normal circadian period.

   a. Irregular sleep-wake rhythm
   b. Advanced sleep phase
   c. Delayed sleep phase

2. ______ disorder happens when a person crosses a lot of time zones in a short period of time.

    a. Shift work

    b. Jet lag

    c. Non 24-hour sleep-wake disorder

3. Women going through menopause often experience
____

    a. Jet lag like symptoms

    b. Hypertension

    c. Insomnia

4. Jet lag is _______ .

    a. Permanent

    b. Temporary

    c. Irrecoverable

5. Night shift workers tend to have ______ body mass index than day shift workers.

    a. Lower

    b. Equal

    c. Higher

B] Answer the following:

1. Distinguish between 'delayed sleep phase disorder' and 'advanced sleep phase disorder'.

2. Write a note on shift-work disorder.

3. What are the causes of disturbed circadian rhythm?

4. Write any four ways to maintain a healthy circadian rhythm.

5. What are the measures to reduce jet lag?

C] Activity:

Maintain sleep dairy and observe the factors affecting sleep quality and quantity

The link for online sleep diary

https://forms.gle/5pSf5TEoxf7XVhrD6

References

- S. M. James, K. A. Honn, S. Gaddameedhi, and H. P. A. Van Dongen, "Shift Work: Disrupted Circadian Rhythms and Sleep Implications for Health and Well-Being," (in eng), Curr Sleep Med Rep, vol. 3, no. 2, pp. 104-112, Jun 2017, doi: 10.1007/ s40675-017-0071-6.

- K. J. Reid and S. M. Abbott, "Jet Lag and Shift Work Disorder," (in eng), Sleep Med Clin, vol. 10, no. 4, pp. 523-35, Dec 2015, doi: 10.1016/j.jsmc.2015.08.006.

- R. L. Sack, "The pathophysiology of jet lag," (in eng), Travel Med Infect Dis, vol. 7, no. 2, pp. 102-10, Mar 2009, doi: 10.1016/j. tmaid.2009.01.006.

- D. B. Boivin and P. Boudreau, "Impacts of shift work on sleep and circadian rhythms," (in eng), Pathol Biol (Paris), vol. 62, no. 5, pp. 292-301, Oct 2014, doi: 10.1016/j.patbio.2014.08.001.

- S. Khan, P. Duan, L. Yao, and H. Hou, "Shiftwork-Mediated Disruptions of Circadian Rhythms and Sleep Homeostasis Cause Serious Health Problems," (in eng), Int J Genomics, vol. 2018, p. 8576890, 2018, doi: 10.1155/2018/8576890.

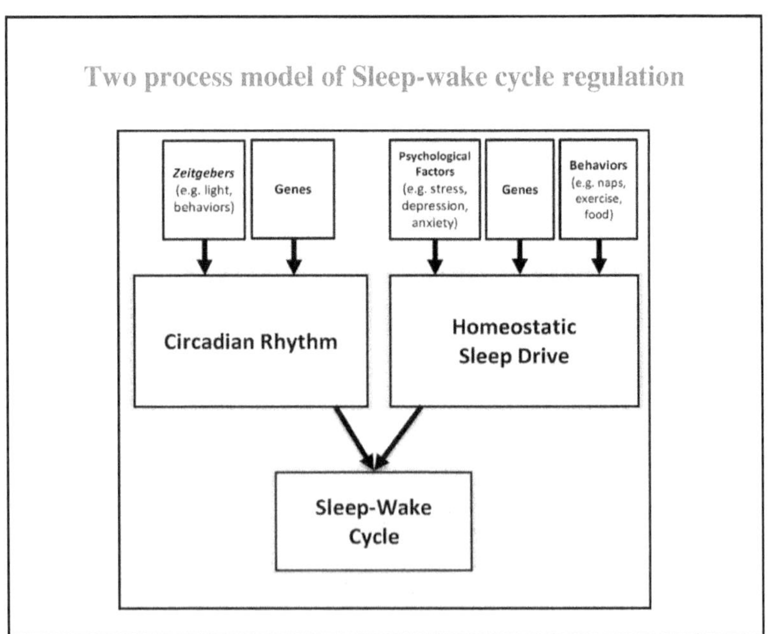

10 CHRONOMEDICINE

Introduction

Circadian rhythms are ruled by body clocks that dictate whether we are alert, sleepy, or hungry and these internal clocks are affected by our environment. The first sign of light sends messages to our bodies to start the arousal process and the setting sun signals the production of melatonin to prepare us for sleep. When we work against body clocks we feel the ill effects - insomnia, lethargy, irritability. In order to perform optimally, we need to work with our circadian rhythms rather than against them. Accordingly if we understand circadian mechanism and suggest medication accordingly, it might be more effective in low doses. This is the idea behind chronomedicine and chronotherapy which is a new form of treatment being investigated in the medical community.

Chronomedicine is an offshoot of chronobiology, the science of understanding body clocks and their resulting biological rhythms along with physiological responses. Chronomedicine is best defined as the application of chronobiology in order to understand the pattern of disease, which can be related to disturbances of circadian rhythm.

Organ clock model

Chronomedicine may be conceptualized as dealing with the prevention, causation, diagnosis and treatment of diseases in humans with a particular focus on the role 'time' plays in our physiology, endocrinology, metabolism and behaviour at many organizational levels. Chronomedicine proposes a better understanding and manipulation of the physiology, using circadian variations as a part of the diagnosis and treatment of certain pathologies. It is the prescribing of medicines at specific clock hours to achieve an optimization of therapeutic administration.

Our biological cycles include certain time points throughout a 24 hour day that allow medicine to have the most beneficial effect while minimizing possible negative side effects. The circadian rhythms fluctuate throughout the day and rhythms of two people are not the same. Therefore it makes sense that treatment should be more individualized and by analyzing the inner workings of our body clocks. Knowledge and familiarity with chronomedicine is emerging within the medical field. It is being investigated for illnesses like asthma, hypertension, some forms of cancer and sleep disorders.

It is also found with chronomedicine, that adverse side effects are limited when the medicine is given at certain circadian stages. For example, when one drug used to treat colon cancer is administered during the night because that is when the diseased cells are the most active, and patient is better able to tolerate the medication during that time. Patients are also able to get treatment via portable pumps designed to release medicine at specific times so that their daily lives are altered as little as possible. Each organ is having small window of optimal performance as shown in figure 17. Though it requires still more experimental support, following diagram gives generalized organ clock model.

Chronotherapy

Researchers in the field of chronobiology have generated sufficient insights regarding the understanding of variations in physiological response in relation with temporal factors. These variations in physiological responses of the body are nowadays utilized for the intervention of therapies and medicines to get their maximum effectiveness, which has evolved as a new therapeutic approach known as chronotherapy.

Chronotherapy involves the administration of medication in coordination with the circadian rhythms of the body to maximize therapeutic effectiveness and minimize or avoid adverse effects. Chronotherapy coordinates biological rhythm with medical treatment. It considers a person's biological rhythms in determining the timing and sometimes the amount of medication to optimize a drug's desired effects and minimize the undesired ones.

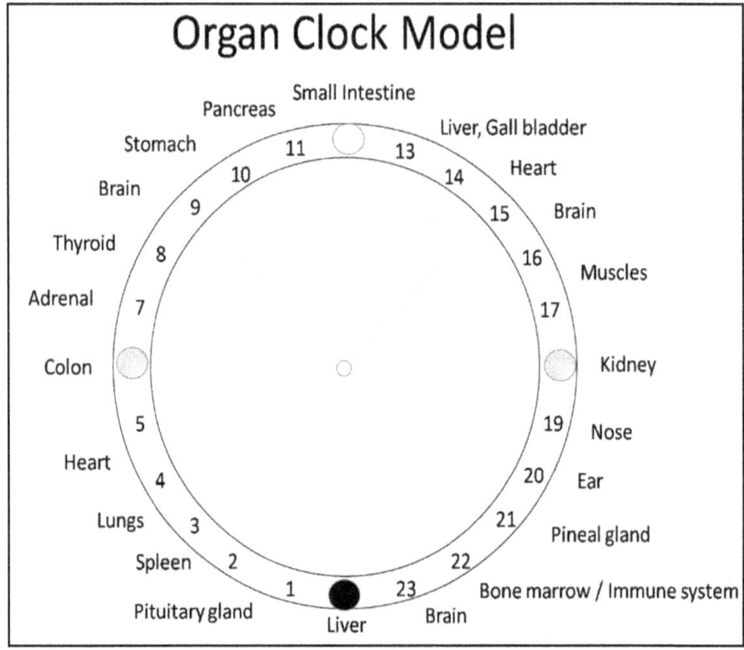

Figure 17: Organ clock model – Chronomedicine prescribes drugs as per the organ clock model to reduce the drug dosage and increase the efficiency.

Chronotherapy works by resetting the circadian clock. This adjustment can relieve widespread problems people have with sleep, depression, jet lag, difficulties linked to shift work, and other lifestyle disorders as well by following interventions.

- Structured light and dark exposure

- Extended wakefulness followed by restorative sleep

- Ultra-low-dose of melatonin

- Meal and/or Exercise timing

Chronotherapeutics

Chronotherapeutics is the discipline concerned with the delivery of drugs according to the intrinsic activities of a disease over a certain period of time. It refers to a treatment method in which in vivo drug availability is timed to match rhythms of disease in order to optimize therapeutic outcomes and minimize side effects. Clinical chronotherapeutics have motivated both the development of programmable-in-time drug delivery pumps and the design of new drug formulations aiming at targeting specific circadian time windows. Few examples are given below.

a) Programmable-in-Time Infusion Pumps – IntelliJect device with four 30-ml reservoirs. Melodie, a second generation of electronically engineered four-channel programmable pumps.

b) Modified Release of Oral Drugs – Controlled pulsatile release capsules of montelukast sodium for the prevention of episodic attack of asthma in the early morning and associated allergic rhinitis.

c) Rhythm-Sensing Drug-Releasing Nanoparticle – Novel nanotechnology-based approaches could link drug release to a relevant molecular circadian rhythm in the cells of interest. This would achieve effective delivery of chronotherapy according to individual patient rhythms independently from drug timing.

Chronotherapy aims to restore circadian time system either by pharmacological or behavioral intervention which is summarized in the figure 18. Behavioral interventions are more effective and long lasting which requires understanding of individual chronotype and optimization of factors that affect the clock mechanism such as light, meal and exercise.

Chronotype

Individual variation in functioning of biological clock is exhibited in the form chronotype. It refers to the idea that there are individual differences in the time of day in which people perform at their peak. In the common vernacular, terms such as "morning person" or "early bird" versus "night person" or "night owl" are reflections of the extreme ends of chronotype.

In biological terms, chronotype refers to the individual difference in preferred timing of sleep and wakeful activity. Both genetic variations and environmental factors influence the distribution of chronotypes in a given population. You may find out your own chronotype with the help of our chronotype questionnaire at link provided below.

https://forms.gle/2Cm5zENLAR1vbMYV8

Research has linked chronotype to performance on cognitive tasks in academic and workplace settings. Studies consistently find that those asked to perform tasks at times that are misaligned with their chronotype show poorer performance than those who perform tasks at more optimal times of the day.

Chronotype analysis will help in various fields such as sports or education or specific professions such as round the clock service industry for performance optimization. More our society will lead to 24x7 lifestyle more will be relevance of chronotype based physical or mental activity in profession or education.

Circadian light /Chrono-light

The solar 24-hour cycle has existed for more than 4 billion years, and it has led to the evolution of circadian rhythms in most organisms. Environmental light is the strongest synchronizer for the circadian system, and phase-resetting capacities of light mainly depend on time of day, light intensity, and spectral composition. Following table illustrates illuminance ranges (lx) under different natural and electrical lighting conditions.

Light exerts acute effects on subjective alertness and cognitive performance, and it inhibits the secretion of melatonin by the pineal gland. Acute light effects are dependent on the photo-pigment melanopsin which is present in the retina of eye and are stronger when light contains a greater proportion of blue light.

Table 3: Light illuminance range

Environmental lighting situation	Typical illuminance range (lux)
Day light, Clear sky	50,000 – 1,00,000
Day light, Overcast sky	10,000 – 20,000
Light therapy lamp	5000 – 10,000
Precise indoor workbench	1000 – 2000
Typical indoor office setting	300 – 500
Living room lighting	50 – 200
Street and Walkway lighting	5 – 20
Full moonlight	<1

Chronobiological knowledge of how light affects human behaviour has begun to be implemented at work places, in schools and in clinical environments. There are still strong experimental evidences required to test, predict and apply optimal lighting conditions for different populations and patients, in terms of spectral composition, light intensity, and dynamics. Also, geographical latitude, building exposure, and building properties play an important role.

Artificial light sources are widely used in our everyday lives to illuminate streets and our homes. There has been a change to use more energy efficient technologies such as light emitting diodes (LEDs) and an increase in the use of digital screens. Artificial lights can vary widely in their brightness and color composition, including how much blue light they emit. These properties, together with the timing and duration of their use, can alter how these light sources may affect health and the environment.

Despite the multitude of studies investigating light effects on humans, it is still unclear how much light is needed during daytime to stay fully entrained to the environmental light-dark cycle. This becomes an important topic in our round-the-clock society, since the time we spend outside during the day progressively decreases, whereas the time we spend with light-emitting devices during the night increases.

Humans have evolved to use daylight and darkness to regulate circadian rhythms, which is important for our health and wellbeing. Increasing exposure to natural daylight, particularly in the morning, can help synchronize the body clock with the solar day. Limiting the amount of light at night is also important for circadian health.

Advances in lighting technology have provided possible ways of reducing adverse lighting effects and enhancing other desired effects. Compared with earlier lighting technologies, LEDs provide precise optical control and more opportunity to change and tune their spectral distribution, allowing lighting designers to reduce obtrusive effects from light scattering into unintended areas.

Chrono-diet / Chrononutrition

A growing body of evidence highlights the importance of the biological clock as a modulator of energy balance and metabolism. It is important to draw a distinction between time restricted feeding and caloric restriction. The former entails the delivery of a certain amount of calories albeit at specific time intervals of specific duration. Calorie restriction entails an overall reduction in caloric intake, albeit without malnutrition. Time restricted delivery of metabolites imposes rhythmic availability of nutrients which resets peripheral clocks in a way that potentially exerts a positive impact on the immune response.

Diet affects many physiological systems including the circadian clocks. The feeding-fasting cycle causes multiple changes such as concentrations of nutrients and microelements in blood and tissues are changed, different hormones are released. In the last few years, there has been increasing recognition of the impact of the biological clock on nutrition, with different effects on energy balance and metabolism and influences on health and diseases. This concept has led to the development of a new discipline known as chrononutrition, which is a research field focused on the study of the interactions between biological rhythms, nutrition, and metabolism. Typically based on chronotype a generalized chronodiet plan is as follows: Three meals a day with 5 hours gap in between and 12 hours gap between dinner and breakfast.

The gut microbiota has emerged as a key factor in metabolic modulation, and its potential influence on circadian rhythms is critical because it regulates the energy derived from food and modulates the levels of host and diet derived products. Thus, changes in the gut microbiota induced by diet can affect the gut clock, influencing the organism's homeostasis. Experimentally it has been demonstrated in mice that gut microbiota composition undergoes circadian oscillations which is dependent on the time and composition of meal.

Different changes in metabolism may be observed in humans based on the consumption of seasonal products due to the particular phenolic profile that the product contains. This fact highlights the need for more such studies focused on the impact of specific phenolic profiles on health that would define more precise dietary recommendations regarding fruits and vegetables.

Chrono-exercise

Among the tissues regulated by clock activity, skeletal muscle represents a major organ system that influences human development as well as aging and disease. Increasing knowledge regarding the circadian clock in humans has indicated that exercise has significant effects in regulating circadian rhythmicity of peripheral clocks.

Altered circadian rhythmicity in skeletal muscle is a cause of concern in our sedentary lifestyle. This impacts reduced glucose tolerance and changes in muscle functioning and composition. These have a significant correlation with conditions such as diabetes, cardiovascular disease, and cancer. Hormonal regulation and resynchronization of the circadian clock as a result of aerobic exercise have each been linked to improved sleep quality, lower heart rate, and lower blood pressure. Skeletal muscle and bone have roles in not only the regulation of locomotion and postural support but also the control of nutritional homeostasis, such as maintaining glucose and calcium levels.

The phase of expression of many rhythmic genes in skeletal muscle occurs at the mid-point of the subjective active phase. Scheduled exercise can entrain the circadian clocks in skeletal muscles that means the phase of rhythmic gene expression in skeletal muscle may be regulated by the rhythm of locomotor activity.

Exercise promotes the production and release of melatonin and commonly results in improved sleep quality though optimal timing still appears to be an open question. Individual sleep patterns can also impact the optimal timing of exercise.

Restoration of circadian time system

Chronomedicine aims at incorporating temporal understanding of body mechanism for disease diagnosis and management. Pharmacological as well as behavioral intervention can restore the circadian time system as summarized in figure 18. It is been successfully incorporated for cancer chemotherapy or asthma management but requires more experimental data to became mainstream in modern medicine   Recommendations of diet, exercise or light exposure would be personalized based on the chronotype analysis which we may expect in futuristic personalized medicine.

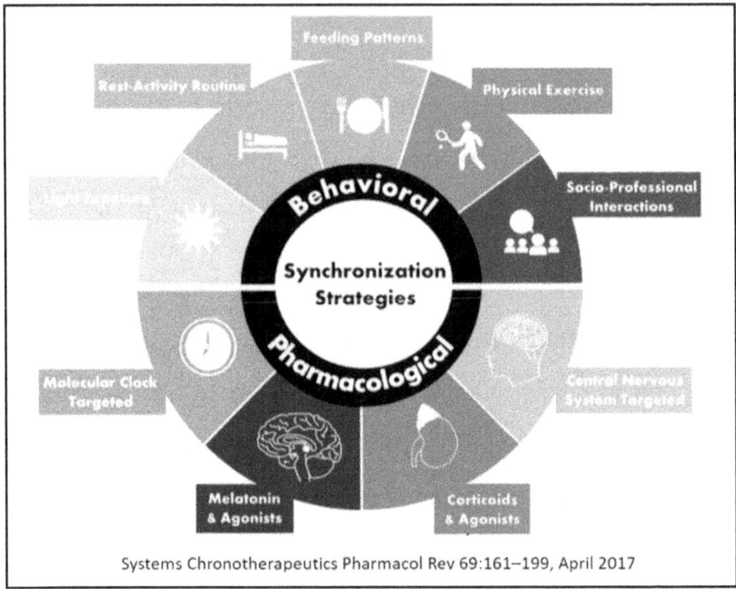

Figure 18: Strategies for restoration of Circadian Time System – CTS restoration may be achieved by either pharmacological or behavioral strategies (Adapted from: Pharmacol Rev 69:161–199, April 2017)

Summary

- Chronomedicine, a new innovative field of physiology and medicine, has emerged, which has greatly improved our understanding of the role of internal clocks for health and diseases.

- The practice of chronotherapy might increase the capability of our body to act better and respond to optimal therapy with larger benefits.

- Chronotherapeutics is the prevention and treatment of diseases based on knowledge of circadian rhythm. It helps in improved diagnosis of diseases by monitoring daily oscillations in vital signs.

- Chronofitness is the emerging concept in the treatment of critical illness which will provide circadian environment with respect to light, feeding and activity for better recovery.

- Chronobiotics are substances that adjust the timing of internal biological rhythms. Many classes of drugs have been claimed to possess such properties (eg. Melatonin).

Exercise

A] Multiple choice questions:

1. '_______' is a behavioral strategy of circadian time system restoration.

   a. Melatonin treatment
   b. Steroid treatment
   c. Feeding pattern scheduling

2. Chronomedicine focuses on the role '________' plays in our physiology.

   a. Time

   b. Date

   c. Period

3. Chronotherapy coordinates ______ with medical treatment.

   a. Diagnosis

   b. Psychology

   c. Biological rhythm

4. ________is a chronobiotic.

   a. Cortisol

   b. Uniphyl

   c. Melatonin

5. Circadian time system can be restored by

   a. Pharmacological intervention

   b. Behavioral intervention

   c. Both of above

B] Answer the following:

1. Define chronomedicine.

2. How is cancer treated with chronomedicine?

3. 'Medical treatment should be more individualized' - Comment.

4. Write a note on 'Chronotherapy'.

C] Activity:

1. Follow chronodiet for 1 month and observe effect on sleep, appetite and overall health.

2. Note down daily exposure of artificial light and correlate the sleep quality and quantity with duration of exposure.

References

- Hower, IM, et al. 2018 Circadian Rhythms, Exercise, and Cardiovascular Health. Journal of Circadian Rhythms, 16(1): 7, pp. 1–8. DOI: https://doi.org/10.5334/jcr.164

- Aoyama S and Shibata S (2017) The Role of Circadian Rhythms in Muscular and Osseous Physiology and Their Regulation by Nutrition and Exercise. Front. Neurosci. 11:63. doi: 10.3389/fnins.2017.00063

- How does blue light affect us? https://www.royalsociety.org.nz/major-issues-and-projects/blue-light-aotearoa

- T. C. Erren et al., "Chronomedicine: an old concept's fledging? A selective literature search," (in eng), Neuro Endocrinol Lett, vol. 33, no. 4, pp. 357-60, 2012.

- L. E. Scheving, "The dimension of time in biology and medicine- -chronobiology," (in eng), Endeavour, vol. 35, no. 125, pp. 66-72, May 1976, doi: 10.1016/0160-9327(76)90030-2.

- R, Kumar & Kumar, Arushi & Sardhara, Jayesh. (2018). Pincal Gland—A Spiritual Third Eye: An Odyssey of Antiquity to Modern Chronomedicine. Indian Journal of Neurosurgery. 07. 001-004. 10.1055/s-0038-1649524.

- Singh, R.K. & Singh, R. & Singh, Vishwajeet & Verma, Narsingh & Singh, Ram & Cornélissen, Germaine. (2016). View point: Chronomedicine. A boon for emerging diseases. World Heart Journal. 8. 65-70.

- M. Münch and A. Kramer, "Timing matters: New tools for personalized chronomedicine and circadian health," (in eng), Acta Physiol (Oxf), vol. 227, no. 2, p. e13300, 10 2019, doi: 10.1111/ apha.13300.

- Chrononutrition and Polyphenols: Roles and Diseases Nutrients 2019, 11, 2602; doi:10.3390/nu11112602

- Annabelle Ballesta et al; Systems Chronotherapeutics Pharmacol Rev 69:161–199, April 2017; https://doi.org/10.1124/pr.116.013441.

11 ADAPTIVE SIGNIFICANCE OF BIOLOGICAL CLOCK

Introduction

Circadian rhythm is a biological process which shows an endogenous and entrainable oscillation of about 24h. These 24h rhythms are regulated by a circadian clock and widely displayed in different organisms including plants, fungi, animals and *Cyanobacteria*. The endogenous circadian rhythms are adjusted to the environment by different surrounding cues such as temperature, light, etc. Ultimately, circadian rhythms are physiological and behavioral changes that follow a daily cycle and influence critical bodily functions such as hormone release, temperature, eating habits, digestion, mood and sleep. Flowering in plants shows a circadian pattern, as does foraging activity in many animals. The ubiquitous nature of circadian rhythms strongly suggests that they confer an adaptive advantage to the organism, in terms of adjusting its physiology and behaviour in anticipation of changes in the environment.

Predictive and Reactive Homeostasis

Changes in the external environment, such as those of weather or atmospheric conditions, can be unpredictable; therefore, organisms need systems that directly respond to changing environments. However, there are also predictable changes which are the result of specific planetary movements such as the day-night cycle (rotation of the earth on its axis), the cycle of the moon (rotation of the earth around the sun). For these predictable changes, organisms have specific mechanisms that generate endogenous biological rhythms corresponding directly to certain periodicities in the environment. They are not directly dependent on the environment but only use the periodic information from the environment to synchronize biological oscillations with cycles of the environment. Thus they are useful for adaptation in the given environmental conditions. For example a lunar tidal rhythm subjects seashore plants and animals to a rhythmic change, typically two high and two low tides occur each day. Many species of shore birds exhibit this rhythm by seeking food only when beaches are exposed to low tides.

The organization of circadian rhythms in animals is flexible. The phase of output rhythms is not enslaved to the phase of the SCN and light–dark cycles alone, but is capable of adjusting to both the experienced and expected environment. Understanding the nature of the flexible timing of output rhythms relative to the SCN might yield important implications for human shift work, chronotherapy, athletic performance and general well-being.

Circadian time-keeping mechanisms enable predictive homeostasis, but the circadian machinery itself can be modulated through principles of reactive homeostasis. This changes the view of the circadian phase from being a rigid response to Zeitgeber stimuli to being an adaptive system that actively reshapes how Zeitgebers are processed depending on homeostatic outcomes and internal states. Reactive mechanisms restore the variable after it goes outside this desired range. Predictive mechanisms adjust the variable before it is expected to go outside this range.

Light and non-photic feedback cues can set the phase of the circadian rhythm generated by the SCN. The phase of peripheral clocks and the timing of behavioral and physiological output rhythms are controlled through multiple mechanisms. The widely accepted view is that daily rhythms are controlled in a hierarchical manner as explained in figure 19. At the top of this hierarchy is the light-entrainable oscillator (LEO) in the SCN, which generates a time-of-day signal capable of entraining the phase of local tissue clocks both in and outside the CNS.

To maximize fitness, animals must optimally interact with their environment in order to maintain homeostatic balance over a prolonged time span. The temporal organization of physiology and behavior are key to successfully maintaining this balance.

The circadian timing of output rhythms is reciprocally linked to homeostasis. If the phenotype is successful, it strengthens the daily routines, leading to a robust phase. By contrast, prolonged failure to maintain homeostatic balance can alter the phase-angle between peripheral clocks and the SCN.

Importance of biological rhythms in humans

Like all other living systems, humans do exhibit all types of biological rhythmicity which is entrained by appropriate environmental cues. There is need to emphasize the importance of circadian lifestyle for modern man who are having more and more artificial ways and means of daily and seasonal activities.

The biological rhythm regulation plays a crucial role in people's healthy lives affected by cosmic events related to the universe and earth. The circadian rhythm works with the mental and physical systems throughout the body. For example, the digestive system produces enzymes to suit the timings of the meals and the endocrine system regulates the hormones to suit normal energy expenditure.

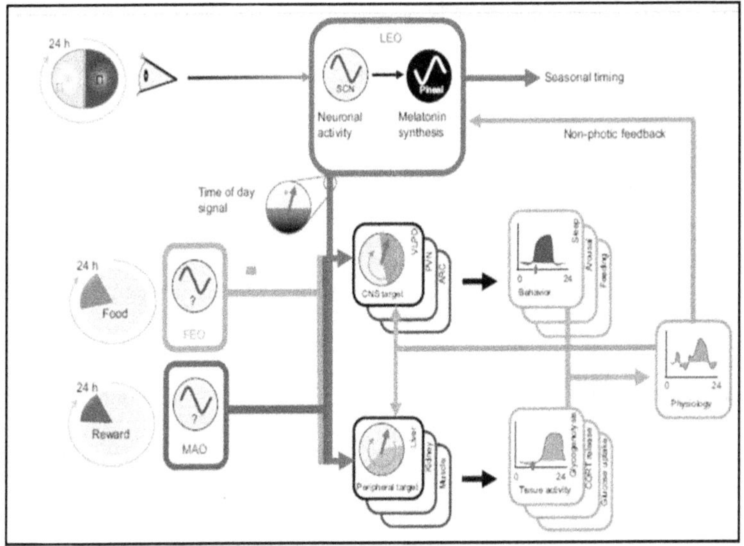

Figure 19: Predictive and Reactive homeostasis - The SCN rhythm directly regulates melatonin synthesis in the pineal gland, which, in turn, is involved in seasonal rhythmicity (red box). Together, neuronal and humoral signals from the SCN and melatonin provide the basis for the time-of-day signal to downstream targets in the brain and body (black boxes). The phase of cellular clocks in these targets relates to rhythmic patterns in behavior and tissue activity (green boxes), collectively inducing daily rhythms in physiological variables (blue box). These physiological rhythms, in turn, provide non-photic feedback to both the SCN and local clocks (blue arrows), which can modulate their phase and accuracy. Timed access to food and rewards (indicated by the orange and purple circle segments, respectively) induces rhythmicity in alternative circadian oscillators – the Food-Entrainable Oscillator (FEO) and the MethAmphetamine-sensitive circadian Oscillator (MAO), respectively. (Adapted from: Journal of Experimental Biology (2017) 220, 738-749 doi:10.1242/jeb.130757)

We know that circadian rhythms are regulated by 'master clock' in the brain. During the day, when we are exposed to sunlight, the master clock sends signals to generate alertness which keeps us awake and active. As night falls, the master clock helps in the production of melatonin - a hormone that promotes sleep and sends signals that helps us to sleep throughout the night. When we sleep well at night, it helps us to be active during the day. In this way, circadian rhythm aligns our sleep and wakefulness with day and night to create a stable cycle of restorative rest that enables increased day time activity.

The clock genes maintain the robust rhythm of 24h in all bodily mechanisms and thus regulate and coordinate internal physiological processes. Brain wave activity, hormone production, cell generation and other important biological processes are determined by circadian rhythm. Circadian rhythms enable humans to better prepare and capitalize on environmental factors such as light and food. Circadian rhythms help maintain many physiological changes that include heart beat rate, production of RBCs and hormones, maintaining body temperature and metabolism as explained in figure 20.

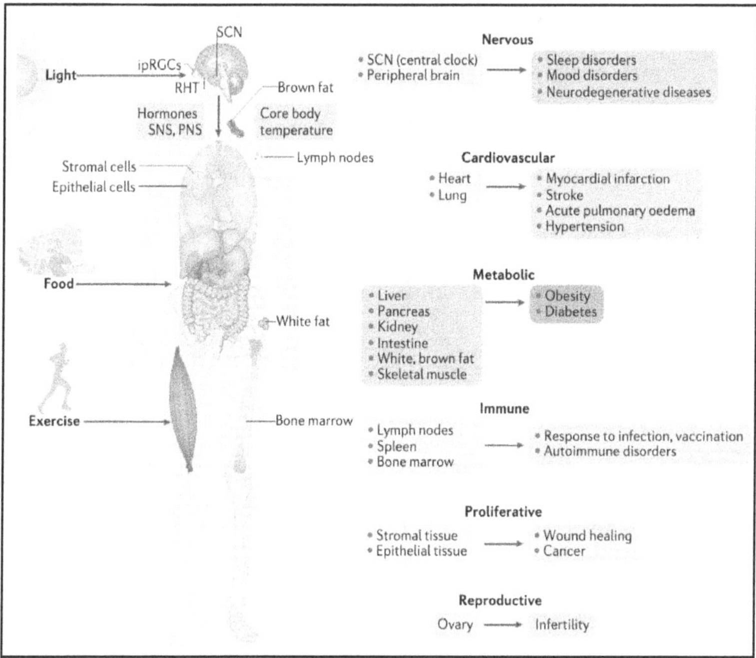

Figure 20: Human Circadian Time System - – Most of the bodily processes are rhythmic in human which are controlled by clock genes. The master clock in SCN regulates and coordinates the circadian time system for optimal adaptation in the given environment along with other non-photic cues such as food and exercise. (Adapted from: Nat Rev Mol Cell Biol. 2020 Feb;21(2):67-84)

Summary

- Circadian lifestyle is a method of devising our day to day life in a healthy manner so as to tune your internal clock mechanism.

- Biological clocks regulate a wide variety of behavioral and metabolic processes in many life forms. They enhance the fitness of organisms by improving their ability to efficiently anticipate periodic events in their external environments, especially periodic changes in light, temperature and humidity.

- Circadian clocks provide fitness advantage. Although the issue of adaptive significance of circadian rhythms has always remained central to circadian biology research, it has never been subjected to systematic and rigorous empirical validation.

- A few studies carried out on free-living animals under field conditions and simulated periodic and aperiodic conditions of the laboratory suggest that circadian rhythms are of adaptive value to their owners.

- Circadian time-keeping mechanisms enable predictive homeostasis, but the circadian machinery itself can be modulated through principles of reactive homeostasis.

Exercise

A] Multiple choice questions:

1. Circadian rhythms are important in regulating internal
   _______ processes.

   a. Physical

   b. Physiological

   c. Signaling

2. Endocrine system regulates hormones to suit ______

   a. Normal energy expenditure

   b. The timings of meals

   c. Both (a) and (b)

3. Circadian rhythms align our ______ and ______ with
   day and night.

   a. Regularities, irregularities

   b. Behavior, lifestyle

   c. sleep , wakefulness

4. Circadian rhythmicity help maintaining ______

   a. Metabolism

   b. Heart beat rate

   c. Both (a) and (b)

5. Mechanism that restore the variable after it goes outside the desired range is called

    a. Reactive homeostasis

    b. Predictive homeostasis

    c. Allostasis

B] Answer the following:

1. How are circadian rhythms useful in adaptation?

2. How are circadian rhythms regulated by 'master clock' in the brain?

3. Explain the importance of circadian rhythms in human physiology.

4. Differentiate between reactive and predictive homeostasis.

C] Activity:

Observe and note down the adaptive behavior in any model organism in two different environmental conditions.

References

- Sunderram et al. Journal of Translational Medicine 2014, 12:79Journal of Experimental Biology (2017) 220, 738-749 doi:10.1242/jeb.130757

- Chrononutrition and Polyphenols: Roles and Diseases Nutrients 2019, 11, 2602; doi:10.3390/nu11112602

- Senthilnathan, Samithamby & Sathiyasegar, Kanthasamy. (2019). Circadian Rhythm and Its Importance in Human Life. SSRN Electronic Journal. 10.2139/ssrn.3441495.

- L. Fuhr, M. Abreu, P. Pett, and A. Relógio, "Circadian systems biology: When time matters," (in eng), Comput Struct Biotechnol J, vol. 13, pp. 417-26, 2015, doi: 10.1016/j.csbj.2015.07.001.

- Patke, A., Young, M.W. & Axelrod, S. Molecular mechanisms and physiological importance of circadian rhythms. Nat Rev Mol Cell Biol 21, 67–84 (2020). https://doi.org/10.1038/s41580-019-0179-2

There is a time to do everything
Time to eat, digestion in top gear 12 noon
Fully fit and wide awake, brain most efficient 10 a.m.-12 noon
Highest pain threshold 8-9 a.m.
Hormones at their peak 7-9 a.m.
The body's systems awaken 6 a.m.
Kidney function at lowest point 5 a.m.
Lungs most active 4 a.m.
Intensive sleep phase 3 a.m.
All systems in regeneration mode except liver and skin 2 a.m.
Dream time 1 a.m.
Afternoon low, time for a nap 1-2 p.m.
New upswing; phase of learning & long term memory 3-4 p.m.
Second peak, best time for manual work 5-6 p.m.
Regeneration and relaxation, optimal sense of smell and taste 6-9 p.m.
Stomach rests – time to stop eating 9 p.m.
Time for bed 11 p.m.
Creativity at its peak 11 p.m.-1 a.m.
http://www.chronobiology.com

LIST OF TABLES AND FIGURES

List of Tables

List of Figures

9 788195 625307